I0792938

CURIOSITIES OF ELMIRA

CURIOSITIES OF ELMIRA

THE LAST LABRADOR DUCK, PROFESSOR SMOKEBALL, THE GREAT FEMALE CRIME SPREE & MORE

KELLI L. HUGGINS

THE History PRESS

Published by The History Press
Charleston, SC
www.historypress.net

Cover images courtesy of Chemung County Historical Society.

Unless otherwise noted, all images in the book appear courtesy of Chemung County Historical Society.

First published 2017

Manufactured in the United States

ISBN 9781467136938

Library of Congress Control Number: 2016956923

For Ted, Sharon, Ted-E and Figaro Huggins for their years of support.

CONTENTS

Contents

ACKNOWLEDGEMENTS

Many people deserve credit for helping me with this project, and surely my attempt at brevity in these acknowledgements will lead me to inadvertently forget to name some of these people. I apologize to and profusely thank anyone I may have neglected.

Thank you to the three editors at The History Press with whom I had the privilege to work: Stevie Edwards, Karmen Cook and J. Banks Smither. Each of you was so tolerant of my many questions and made the process of writing my first book as painless as possible.

A special thank-you to Dr. Jennifer Dorsey, who I am fortunate to call my mentor and my friend. It was on her recommendation that this project even began, and I am forever grateful for her honesty and support.

Thank you to my colleagues at the Chemung County Historical Society: Erin Doane, Rachel Dworkin, Christine Gunderson and Bruce Whitmarsh. Not only are they experts in the field who have pushed me to learn more and do better, but they also routinely tolerate my ridiculous lines of historical inquiry. They offered valuable feedback at all steps in this project. The expansive collections at the historical society formed the basis for this book, and it is a delight to my nerdy heart to have daily access to such historical treasures.

Bridget Sharry read a nearly final draft of this manuscript and used her characteristic wit and honesty to help me eliminate the phrases that did not sound like "me."

I spent time in the Elmira College Archives at the Gannett-Tripp Library looking at the Elizabeth "Bessie" Hotchkiss collection, and I thank the archivist and curator, Nathaniel Ball, for his assistance. I would also like to thank everyone who works tirelessly behind the scenes, digitizing newspapers for websites like the New York State Historic Newspapers project, Chronicling America and Fultonhistory.com. As a historian whose work depends on newspapers, I am able to reconstruct the narratives of many of the people and events in this book only because of this digital accessibility.

Finally, thank you to my family. They all deserve credit for encouraging my interest in history from a young age. My grandmother Ann Shoemaker read an early draft, and I value her feedback. My mother, Sharon, has carried the brunt of my historical burden, however, and she has endured (and, I dare say, *mostly* enjoyed) countless hours of reading various papers and articles and listening to me babbling about the minutia of drama that occurred well over one hundred years ago.

INTRODUCTION

When I moved to Elmira in 2013, I knew the basics of the local history. Stories like those of Mark Twain's summers in Elmira, the Elmira Civil War Prison Camp and Elmira College are well known. But as I worked on exhibits, blog posts, articles and other projects, I began compiling more and more stories of lesser-known figures and events. For a historian, Elmira is an ideal location to study. This small city has had a progressive and prosperous spirit throughout its history that has allowed the people highlighted in this book to reach heights of fame or infamy.

I like to think of this book, and my work in general, as serving to champion the historically forgotten. One of the cruel realities of historical practice is that we are unable to remember everyone. In many cases, documentation simply does not exist to tell us about some lives in the past. In other cases, the stories have been forgotten, replaced in public memory by those more current, memorable or notable. This happens especially to the historically disenfranchised: minorities, women, people with disabilities or illnesses and even nonhuman animals. And, as this book shows, even people who were internationally famous during their lifetimes can be forgotten. So, in part, this book is an attempt to bring just a small fraction of these people back into our historical conversations. As we talk about Mark Twain, let us also reserve some time to discuss Bob Mack, Henry Clum, Bessie Hotchkiss, Lew Gilmore, Mary Fairman, Bob the Sea Lion and others.

Most of these stories took place in the same era, so it is fun to remember that many of the people in this book were aware of and interacted with others also mentioned. These intersections serve as a reminder that, as is the case today, Elmira was vividly interconnected. Some people operated in the same elite social circles; others occupied the same jail cells. Local newspapers were filled with their exploits. Page five of the Sunday, January 11, 1891 edition of the *Elmira Telegram*, for example, featured stories about Jean Hotchkiss, Mary Fairman and the LaFrance brothers. In a more macabre connection, the final resting place of many of the people discussed in this book is Elmira's beautiful Woodlawn Cemetery.

My favorite perk of being a historian is that there is always something new to learn. There is always another person to discover or event to reconstruct. I hope that readers approach this book, other historical works and even their own research with the same curiosity.

PART I

INNOVATIVE INVENTORS

Elmira has long been the home of smart, creative people who have sought new solutions to a range of questions and problems. These scientific pioneers have worked in a variety of fields and have many patents to their names. The following stories highlight just a few of these people. In fields ranging from meteorology to agricultural science to rocketry, these men made Elmira a recognized scientific center.

1

HENRY CLUM

Henry Clum was a scientific visionary. Reclusive and eccentric, Clum was more comfortable with his experiments and inventions than with people. His life was marked by tragedy but also great achievement. Although now largely forgotten, he was one of the first meteorologists.

Henrich Augustus Clum was born on August 17, 1821, in Clermont, Columbia County, New York. His parents, Jacob and Elisabeth Schultes Clum, had ten children, and the family lived in poverty. Because of the family's dire finances, young Henry had little formal schooling. Instead, he became a tailor's apprentice at age thirteen. The tailor was a drunk and a gambler, and Henry ran away from him three times. The Clum family moved to western New York, settling first in Wayne County in 1840. Henry continued to work as a tailor.

Despite having a stable trade, Henry Clum was a dreamer. Later in life, he relished telling the story of how, as a child, he was institutionalized in an insane asylum near LeRoy, New York, for claiming to be able to predict the weather—an outlandish claim at the time. Clum was deemed sane and released after a week. Whether or not he was ever actually institutionalized, he did demonstrate precocious scientific ability. He began experimenting as a young man and took some classes at the Brockport Collegiate Institute.

By the late 1840s or early 1850s, "aerial locomotive" company Porter and Robjohn employed Clum to tour the region, giving lectures and demonstrations of their invention. This was Clum's introduction to public scientific demonstrations, and it provided crucial experience he would need when he began showing his own work.

Clum's life as a young scientist was difficult. He made what money he could by teaching and lecturing, but he lived in deep poverty. He later claimed that during this time he did not own a bed; instead, he "slept on a piece of carpet spread on the floor of his unfurnished room with another piece of carpet for covering."[1] He funneled all of his spare money into his inventions.

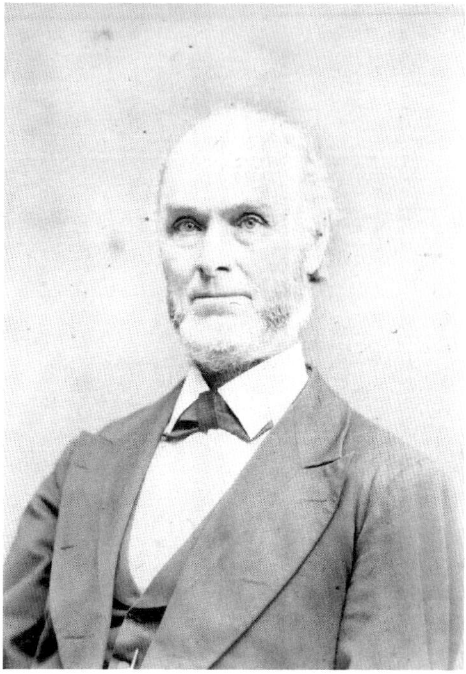

Portrait of Henry Clum.

By the 1860s, Clum had received several patents for his work. He invented a scale for improved weighing and measuring. In 1860, while living in Auburn, New York, he patented his first barometer. This barometer was innovative in its ability to take accurate readings at various altitudes, producing more reliable results. His work with this instrument set the stage for his greatest achievement.

In 1861, Clum patented a new type of barometer that he dubbed the "Aelloscope," named for the Greek words for "storm" and "view." He formed the American Aelloscope Company in Rochester, New York, to help promote his work. The instrument was the culmination of twenty-five years of work studying weather and atmospherics. The complex machine consisted of gas chambers connected to a column with sixty to two hundred pounds of mercury. As the mercury levels fluctuated with changes to atmospheric pressure, a buoy moved, noting the shifts. The gas chambers added to the accuracy of the mercury readings.

Beyond the improved accuracy, Clum claimed that his Aelloscope was "read as easily as a clock or watch, even to the one-thousandth or two-thousandth part of an inch."[2] Readability was a key feature of the machine, because Clum wanted his invention to be used by the wider public, not just by trained scientists. The machine's aesthetics were also a selling point. Discussing the instrument's beauty, James D. Reid, secretary of the American Aelloscope Company, wrote that it would be "a welcome addition to the finest library, or the most elaborately ornamented parlor or drawing room; and while it will be in keeping with these, it will be equally so in the halls of public institutions or on the lawns of private or public estates."[3] The company planned to sell several versions of the machine, varying in size and price. Prices would range from $1,000 to $10,000. In its largest size, the Aelloscope measured ten feet tall and weighed nearly one ton.

Clum and the American Aelloscope Company had grand plans for the machines. They believed that the Aelloscopes could be used to predict large weather events and, therefore, save lives. If potentially disastrous storms could be forecast, maritime accidents could be averted. In its promotional circular, the company outlined a plan for a central office that would accept Aelloscope readings from around the world via telegraph lines. The firm believed that a processing and computing station could take the readings from fifty of the instruments positioned across North America and send the results to lighthouses and ports in the path of storms.[4]

A fully operational Aelloscope could allegedly detect changes in atmospheric pressure from thousands of miles away. In October 1862, the Aelloscope was in Rochester when it began detecting pressure changes that a standard barometer next to it did not. No signs of bad weather were perceived by people, but after six days of movement on the instrument, a violent storm passed through Washington, D.C., and up to Pennsylvania. That storm was the first that the Aelloscope detected. In 1864, Clum's Aelloscope in Rochester and the Aelloscope of Dr. T.D. Prichard in Phelps, New York, had the same readings, predicting a storm in the western states. The American Aelloscope Company's circular provided other testimonials to illustrate that the instrument, while still in its infancy, was proving successful.

Clum likely moved to Elmira in the late 1860s, continuing his work promoting the Aelloscope. Around this time, he began doing demonstrations in Europe, including some for royalty and heads of state. He sold Aelloscopes to Queen Victoria of England, Napoleon III of France and the Russian government. E.R. Hammatt, president of the American Aelloscope Company, went to the 1867 Paris Universal Exhibition to display the instrument. A correspondent for the *New York Times* provided a detailed description of the strange-looking contraption: "At first sight, it looks like an elaborate soda-water fountain, or a bundle of pontoons, or a complicated tea urn, or a dry gas meter. A person of a lively imagination could guess at it for a day without finding out what it was."[5] Despite the machine's

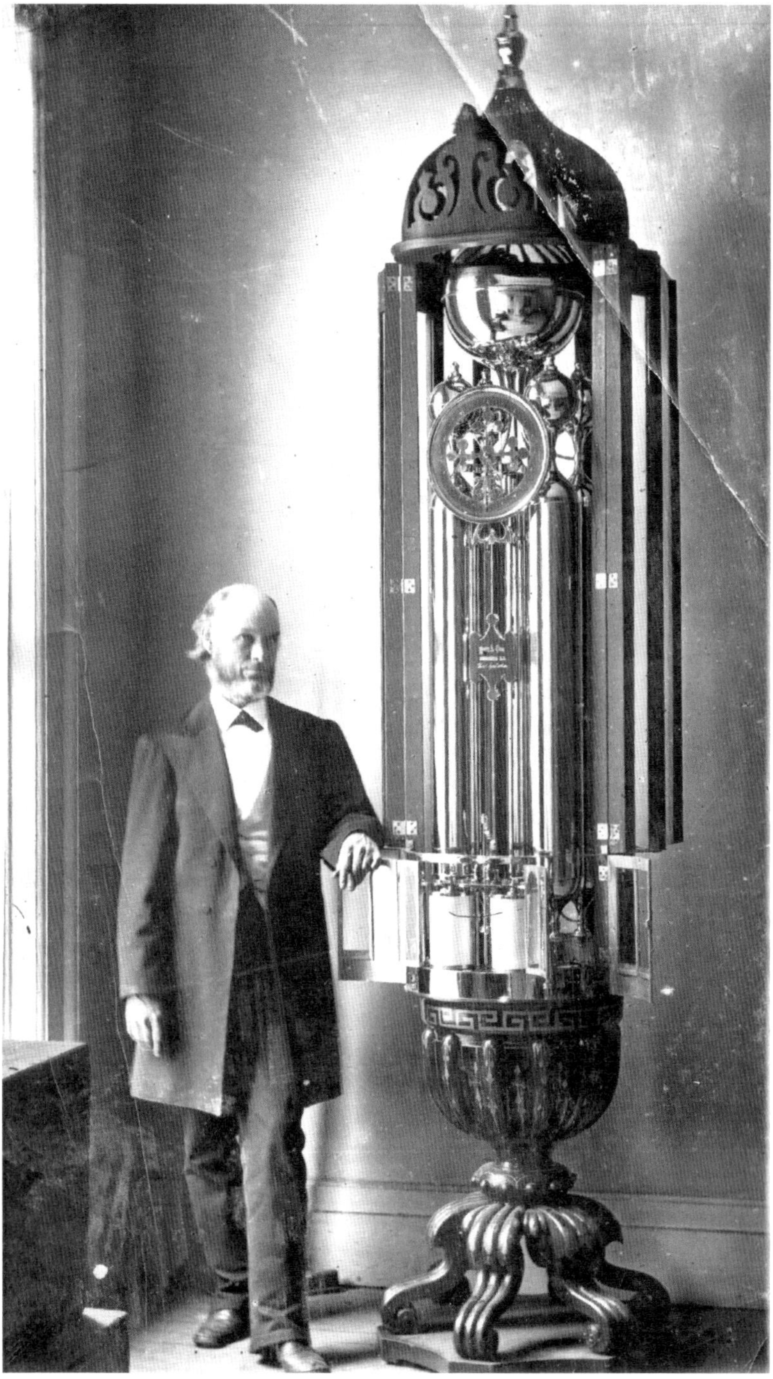

Henry Clum with his Aelloscope.

puzzling appearance, the reviewer was convinced that it was a significant advancement in meteorological science.

Clum sold some of his Aelloscopes in the United States, too. The *New York Tribune* used one for its weather forecasting. Senator Charles Sumner talked to Clum about perching one atop the U.S. Capitol building, but after Sumner died, the plans were cancelled. The American government ultimately did purchase one. The machine needed to be taken apart and cleaned every year, and by the second year, the machine's owners thought that they could do it themselves, without Clum's assistance. They were not able to put the complicated Aelloscope back together, and when they requested Clum's assistance, he refused, claiming he did not take secondhand work.

Despite Clum's successes, aelloscopy proved a difficult business from which to profit. Clum sold few of his machines, mostly due to their high cost. After the Paris exhibition, one reviewer of the Aelloscope reported, "as its superiority to the ordinary barometer seems doubtful, while its cost is immensely greater, the commercial success of the invention must be questionable."[6] Clum was offered $10,000 for the rights to his patent, but he refused. He believed his life's work to be worth no less than $100,000. A newspaper joked that if his attempts to sell the machine to the scientific community failed, Clum could "make his everlasting fortune of intending bridal parties and women with new bonnets." Ultimately, he derived little income from the sale of his Aelloscope and instead made his meager living from lectures and the sale of his smaller barometers.

Clum lived in poverty and was largely reclusive. He married Annie Snell, an Elmiran who was the widow of Charles Harris. The Clums were happily married for five years and had a daughter. Their domestic life was destroyed, however, when Harris, who had reportedly died in the Civil War, came back to Elmira to reclaim his wife. Annie went to Buffalo with her first husband, taking Clum's daughter with her. As he had done before, Harris left Annie while they were in Buffalo. Clum and Annie never remarried, though he did financially support her and his daughter until Annie died in 1881. Clum even covered her burial expenses.

Besides his brief relationship with Annie, Clum had only one other close friend and confidant. Matt Lockwood was the costumer for Elmira's Lyceum Theater, near where Clum lived. The two men shared many common interests. They talked about astronomy and identified constellations. Clum shared his ideas about religion, claiming that the inspiration for his Aelloscope came from the Bible. Lockwood was one of the few people who was able to understand and put together the Aelloscope.

Throughout the 1870s and early 1880s, Clum continued his work in aelloscopy, but he also pursued other inventions and interests. He maintained a fascination with the prospect of flight, a holdover from his early career lecturing about blimps. He believed that if he found a patron, he would be able to make significant advances in the field. Clum lamented that the public perception of aviation was "injured by the futile attempts of brainless enthusiastics to fly with wings." Writing of his goals for the field of aviation, he said, "I hope to live not only to see my cherished idea of Aellography established throughout the world, but also to be able to break the fast with our enterprising locals in Elmira, and to break the necks of champagne bottles with the same worthies in Boston, Washington or Chicago at the dinner table the same day."[7] Some of his other work took still different forms. In 1878, he patented a portable commode for use in hospitals and nurseries. The functional piece doubled as a fashionable ottoman that was supposed to keep odors to a minimum.

On July 6, 1884, Clum was scheduled to give a lecture at the Fireman's Hall in Binghamton, New York. As he prepared for his talk later that day, one of the pieces of equipment, probably for the projector, exploded. The blast broke the windows of the hall and sent iron shrapnel flying. One piece struck Clum in the back of the head, killing him. He was alone in the hall, so no one else was injured. One of Clum's prized Aelloscopes was on the stage of the hall at the time of the explosion. Remarkably, it was not damaged. Matt Lockwood came to Binghamton to bring his friend's body back to Elmira. Upon his arrival, Lockwood discovered that the people in Binghamton were planning to keep the Aelloscope. Enraged, he waited until everyone left the hall and stole it out of Binghamton.

Clum was buried in the Lockwood family plot in Woodlawn Cemetery. A few friends and his daughter attended the funeral. While he was not able to see aelloscopy achieve worldwide recognition during his lifetime, his work contributed to advancements in meteorology.

2

TRUCKSON AND ASA LaFRANCE

LaFrance is still a recognizable name in Elmira, even though the American LaFrance Fire Engine Company factory in the city closed in 1985. The company employed generations of Elmirans, and the fire engines produced there were internationally renowned. While the modern history of the company is fresh in the minds of many, the origins are more complex and distant. The success of the company was greatly indebted to the work of two brothers: Truckson and Asa LaFrance.

Truckson and Asa were descended from French Huguenot immigrants who changed their name from Hyenveux to LaFrance when Americans struggled to pronounce the distinctive surname. Born in Braintrim, Pennsylvania, on September 14, 1834, Truckson was ten years older than Asa, who was born on March 21, 1844. Their parents, Willis and Clarissa, had three other sons and at least three daughters.

Truckson came to Elmira in 1850 and worked in a foundry. He married Elmiran Harriet Burgess on January 12, 1859. A mechanical genius with a particular interest in engines and motors, Truckson patented a piston fob steam engine in 1860. Anecdotes illustrate his innate knack for understanding machinery. For example, at some point in the early 1860s, the new printing press at the office of the *Daily Advertiser* newspaper broke, and Truckson offered a solution to the frustrated owners. Incredulous, they asked him what experience he had with such machines. Truckson admitted he had none, but they allowed him to try, and he was able to fix it. He was offered a job and worked at the newspaper for a couple of years. He also served as an engineer for the local fire department, which inspired his later work.[8]

Younger brother Asa had other interests. A gifted musician, Asa specialized in the E-flat cornet and played in brass bands. He was a member of the First New York Veteran Cavalry during the Civil War and became its bandleader. After his service, he returned to Elmira and worked as a professional musician. In 1862, Asa was in a serious hunting accident. He tried to climb a fence, and his loaded gun went off into his left arm. The bone was so badly shattered that Dr. William C. Wey had to amputate Asa's arm at the shoulder. The press reported, "Young LaFrance is, of course, very much prostrated, but it is hoped he will recover."[9]

Asa's disability did not hold him back professionally. In the 1860s, he traveled with several bands and vaudeville troupes, including Cal Wagner's Minstrels and De Coo's Great New Orleans Burlesque Opera Troupe and Brass Band. He formed the Asa LaFrance Band in 1868.

The sixteen-piece LaFrance Band found great success around the region in the late 1860s and the 1870s, due in large part to its charismatic leader. In reminiscences of the band printed decades later, the former members spoke fondly of Asa's leadership and enthusiasm. Charles Roosa wrote:

> *We played for something beside the dollars we received in those little envelopes that Asa used to hand around at the rehearsals….Asa was full of enthusiasm and imparted his spirit to the whole organization. There was an unconscious something about our little leader that we all felt, but never were conscious of feeling.*

And Asa was a resourceful bandleader. Printed band music was expensive, so he would write the parts for the entire ensemble himself.[10]

The brass band toured extensively, performing at political rallies, parades and other events. Asa frequently stole the show at these gatherings. One former member recalled:

> *Playing at a political meeting in Breesport…Asa played one of his triple-tongue solos, and after the applause had died down, an old big farmer jumped up and swinging his old hat, shouted: "Three cheers for the little one-armed boy what leads the band."*[11]

In another instance, the band was playing in Auburn, New York, and was asked to play during the judging interlude of a local battle of the bands contest. It agreed, and its performance brought the house down. Reportedly, "An old husky-voiced farmer arose from his seat, and above all the applause, cried out so you could almost hear him all over the building: 'I vote to give the little one arm cuss all the prizes.'"[12]

While Asa was busy touring with the LaFrance Band, Truckson started the LaFrance Manufacturing Company with his business partner, John Vischer, in 1873. The prominent Diven family financially backed the endeavor and held leadership positions in the company. They purchased ten acres of land to build the necessary factory space. This included a machine shop, brass foundry, pattern room, blacksmith shop, engine room and molding room. The company manufactured a variety of mechanical goods, including corn shellers and steam locomotives, but it soon began to specialize in steam fire engines.

As the company grew, so did Truckson's need for a good salesman. His personable, showman brother Asa was a perfect fit for the job. In 1876, Asa joined the company as a traveling salesman. This new gig interfered with his band leadership duties. One time, Asa had to abandon his troupe shortly before a show because he needed to go to Alabama to do a product demonstration. In a bid to raise the spirits of the band members and get on with the show, cornet player Charlie Geer pretended to be Asa, tucking his left arm in his jacket all day. He successfully fooled the crowd.[13]

Asa traveled regionally and nationally with the company's engines, giving demonstrations and selling products. His affable personality won him admirers. During a demonstration in Port Jervis, New York, an impressed reporter wrote, "He seems to be a gentleman in every sense of the word, and is well known by a number of musical friends."[14] In 1878, the brothers sent their engine to the Paris exposition, hoping an international stage would increase their sales. However, they neglected to check the French laws regulating boilerplate thickness before submitting their machine and shipping it across the Atlantic Ocean. The machine did not comply and could not be displayed. This incident almost bankrupted the business.

The company did manage to rebound from the Paris debacle. Truckson continued to patent engine and boiler improvements. With the support of financier Thomas Hotchkiss, the company built the "Jeanie Jewell," an engine named after Hotchkiss's wife. Asa brought the machine to Chicago, Illinois, and Waterloo, Iowa, for competitions. The machine won, which helped boost sales of LaFrance engines.

On February 17, 1881, Asa wed Emma Haviland. They were married by Reverend Thomas K. Beecher, and the LaFrance band played the wedding

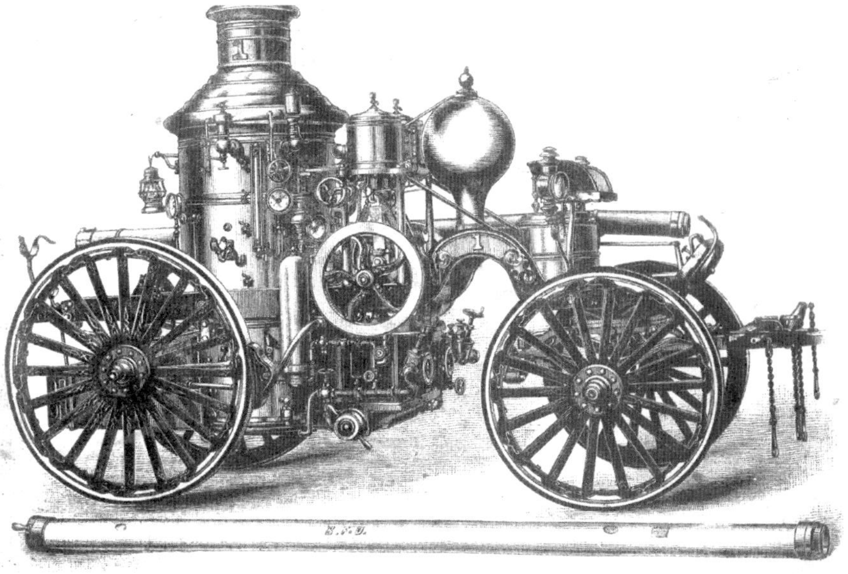

Illustration of a LaFrance horse-drawn engine, circa 1888.

march. Asa decreased his activity with the band, eventually retiring as its leader. He turned his focus fully toward the company.

In 1882, the company worked with Daniel D. Hayes to manufacture his eighty-five-foot-long truck extension ladder. The revolutionary piece of equipment was significantly longer than any other on the market. In 1884, the company made its first piston steam engine, which was sold to the Buffalo Fire Department. Asa continued to travel and promote the firm's inventions.

Truckson kept innovating. In 1891, he invented a new fire engine pump, which used an "entirely new principle" to deliver more water pressure. The invention caused the *Elmira Telegram* to proclaim, "Elmira is destined to be the center of the fire engine building industry of the United States." Truckson negotiated with the company, stating that he would remain with it as long as he got $100 in royalties for each engine built for the next thirty years.[15] He received a patent for his tubular steam boiler the next year.

Truckson died suddenly on September 16, 1895, from "paralysis of the heart." He had gone for a walk and developed stomach pains. When the pains did not cease when he laid down, he went to see a nearby doctor. He sat down in a chair in the doctor's office and died. His obituary read, "His death is a serious loss in business circles as well as to his family and friends....His honor and worth won the respect and affection of all who knew the man."[16] The company continued on. In 1895, Truckson received a posthumous patent for the pump valve he designed. Asa patented an elevating screw for fire engine ladders in 1898.

Significant changes were coming. In 1900, the LaFrance Fire Engine Company merged with the American Fire Engine Company to create the International Fire Engine Company. The American Fire Engine Company itself was the result of an 1891 merger of four smaller fire engine manufacturers. The 1900 merger added not only the LaFrance company but also other fire engine, equipment and extinguisher companies. This new monopoly changed its name to the American LaFrance Fire Engine Company in 1904. The company had its headquarters in New York City before moving to Elmira in 1906.

Asa stayed with the company initially, even inventing a new ladder and boiler.[17] But in July 1905, he and Charles R. Moore left the American LaFrance Fire Engine Company. They had recently patented engine pumps and boilers but could not come to a satisfactory agreement with American LaFrance for the purchase of the designs. After almost thirty years in his family's trade, Asa left the fire engine business.[18]

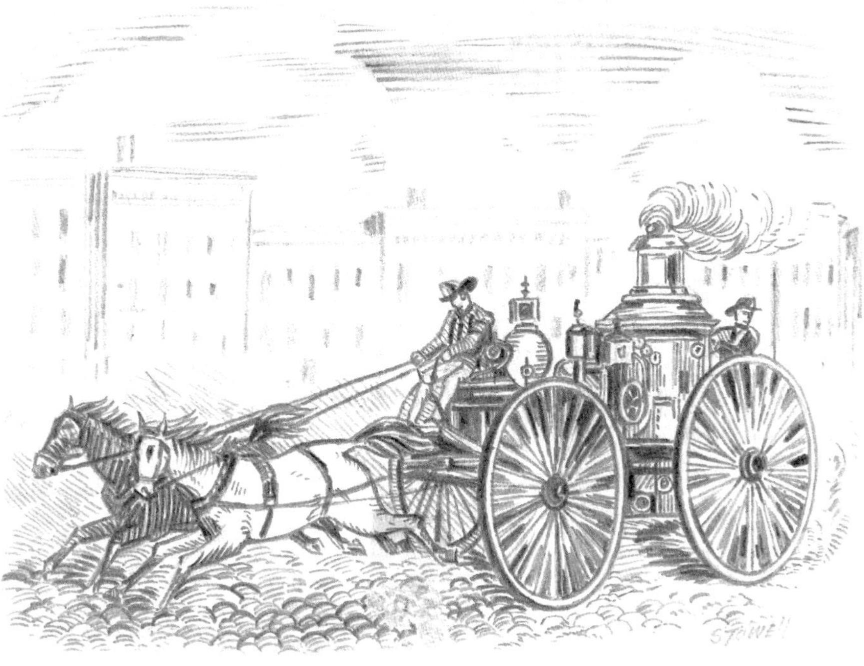

Drawing of a LaFrance fire engine in use.

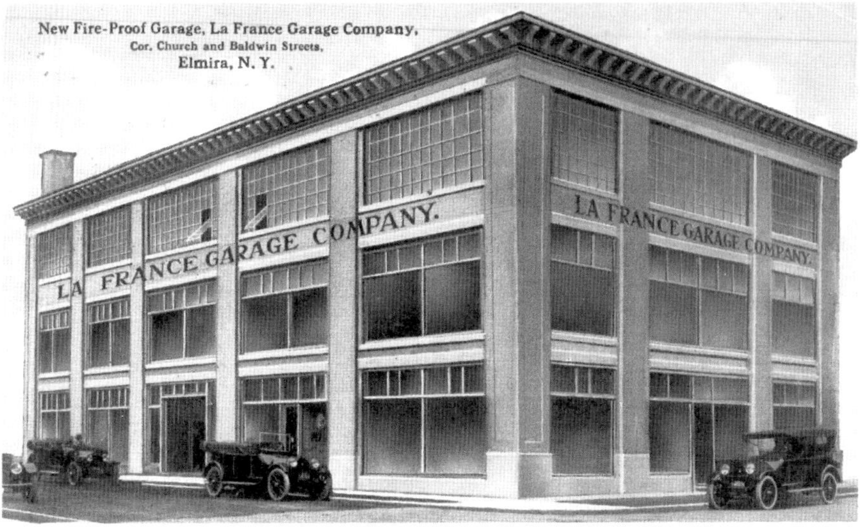

Postcard showing the LaFrance Garage Company.

Embracing a new venture, Asa opened the LaFrance Motor Car Company and began selling automobiles and supplies. Working with his sons Coleman and A. Ward, Asa found success as a dealer of Chalmers and several other types of cars. Ever the showman, in July 1911, he challenged famed aviator Lincoln Beachey to a race between Beachey's airplane and one of Asa's Chalmers Forty cars.[19] Beachey accepted the challenge, and his plane won. Asa also took part in various other automobile races.

In the 1900s or 1910s, Asa made another foray into the fire engine business, forming the Asa LaFrance Fire Engine Company. This company was not associated with American LaFrance. It specialized primarily in steam engine repairs. The company dissolved in June 1914 as the demand for steam engines slowed with the increasing use of gasoline.[20] Asa then formed the LaFrance Garage Company with his sons.

Asa retired from his company in March 1916; he had become increasingly ill with "hardening of the arteries."[21] His sons A. Ward and Coleman were promoted to president and vice president, respectively.[22] Asa died on January 23, 1927, after a long illness.

The LaFrance legacy lived on long after Truckson and Asa. Asa's son A. Ward formed the Ward LaFrance Truck Company in Elmira. American LaFrance continued operations in Elmira until 1985. The plant moved to Virginia and, later, to South Carolina. American LaFrance closed for good in 2014 due to financial struggles.

3

THE PHILO NATIONAL POULTRY INSTITUTE

The grand building at 1575 Lake Street has housed several businesses since it was completed in 1909, but none has been as unique as the first. Edgar Woodruffe Philo was an innovator in the field of poultry farming, and his Philo National Poultry Institute, housed in that building, was at the center of a great change in the business of egg production. Philo devised a new system involving chickens being housed in close confinement. Although confinement is common in modern industrial agriculture, in the early twentieth century, the notion was radical and contradicted centuries of practice. For the most part, improvement in the field during this era was done at agricultural colleges or experiment stations, but some amateurs, like Philo, also made an impact on the industry. Agricultural journals were an outlet for the dissemination of poultry knowledge and offered a venue for businessmen like Philo to advertise their ideas.

Philo, born in 1863, began experimenting with poultry technology long before he moved to Elmira or opened his institute. As a boy, he began caring for chickens, and that interest led him to start his own day-old chick sales business. It was with this early business venture that Philo discovered the secret to his later success. One day, young Philo's chicks outnumbered the necessary heating lamps and coop space for their care. He was forced to leave the chicks in cramped, unheated conditions, and he expected them to be dead the next morning. To his surprise, the chicks were still alive the next day and appeared to be doing better than those under the lamps. Philo, recognizing the importance of this discovery, decided to pursue it further.[23]

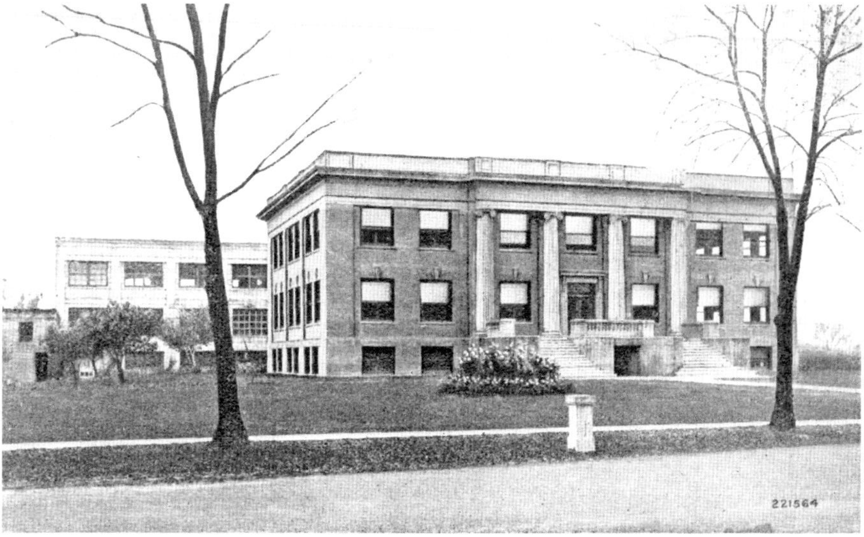

Postcard showing the Philo National Poultry Institute.

By 1887, he was living in New York State's Capital District, where he invented an apparatus in which alcohol was used to regulate temperature in incubators.[24] He acquired a patent for his first egg incubator design in 1903. Philo did this with no formal agricultural schooling.

Philo founded the Cycle Hatcher Company, which produced "fireless," or unheated, brooding and hatching equipment. He moved to Elmira in 1906, bringing his company with him. The Elmira Chamber of Commerce had been actively courting businesses to relocate to the city, and Philo found the commercial climate a good fit for his company.[25] The firm sold hatchers around the world, with orders coming from as far away as Buenos Aires, Argentina, and Johannesburg, South Africa.

Philo also began printing his own agricultural journal, *The Poultry Review*, in which he and others wrote articles about poultry keeping and the Philo system. The journal also served to advertise the Cycle Hatcher Company and other business endeavors. By 1911, Philo claimed that the *Review* had a readership of over 100,000 people in the United States and in more than thirty countries.

Philo's writing was not limited to the *Review*. In 1907, he published *The Philo System of Progressive Poultry Keeping*. In it, he fully outlined his ideas about poultry keeping, claiming that those of his contemporaries were "without foundation." The Philo system was far more complex than other poultry

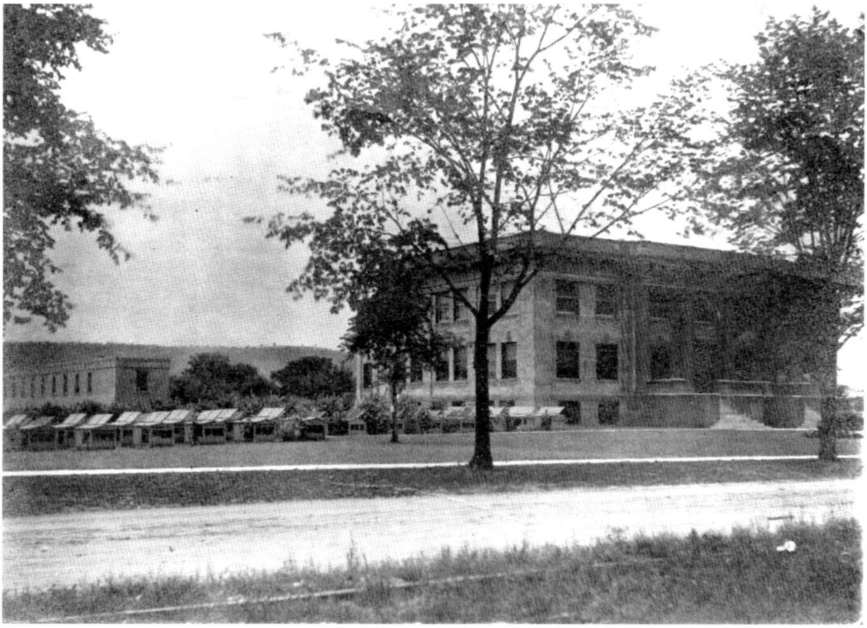

Photograph postcard of the Philo National Poultry Institute, showing Philo coops on the left.

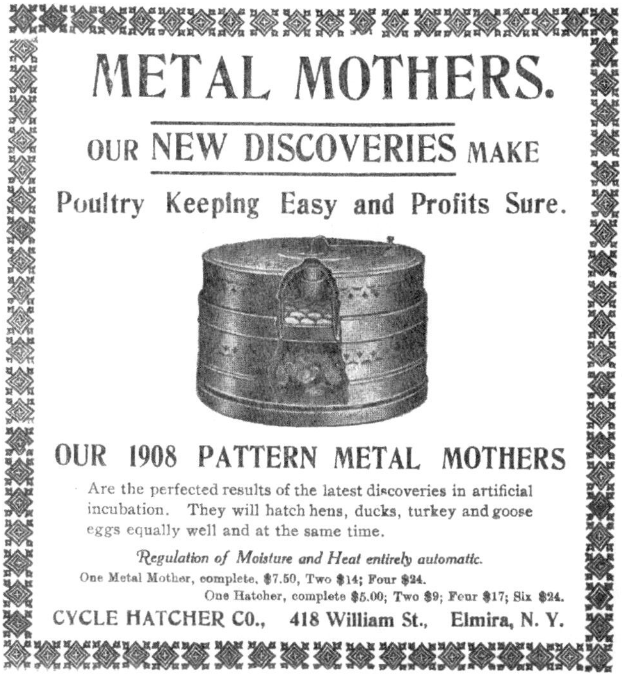

Advertisement for "Metal Mother" incubators from the Cycle Hatcher Company.

care methods; his instructions for the care of the birds had sixteen steps and took all day. The book also fully described his theories that chickens should be raised without artificial heat and that close confinement was best. Philo claimed that "when they [chicks] come into the world they are supplied with an abundance of heat and all we have to do is retain it."[26] Philo also objected to artificial heat on anti-industrial grounds, arguing that when people "endeavored to devise appliances whereby the chickens may be turned out like the output of great factories," nature would have "something to say when its laws are violated."[27]

Philo argued that his system of small enclosures, with no more than three square feet of space per bird, was best for chickens. In addition to maintaining necessary warmth in the absence of heat lamps, confinement protected hens from some of the dangers they would face if they were allowed to roam free. Free-range chickens ate too many insects, he argued, which was bad for their digestion. The diets of Philo's chickens could be closely monitored for optimal growth.[28] The book provided instructions for constructing coops that complied with the Philo system.

Philo had the thirty-thousand-square-foot building on Lake Street constructed for his National Poultry Institute in 1909. The building and the surrounding thirty-acre plot housed his multiple poultry businesses and increased his offerings. The new space allowed Philo to expand his printing operations. He produced the *Review*, his books, advertisements and other materials on the first floor of the building. Visitors could peruse the model coops set up on the institute's grounds, and laboratories allowed Philo to continue experimenting. By 1913, he had received six patents for his special coops and "fireless" brooders. The *Reliable Poultry Journal* called the institute building "THE LARGEST, MOST COSTLY AND MOST IMPOSING STRUCTURE THAT EVER HAS BEEN ERECTED ON THE PLANET EARTH FOR THE PURPOSE OF POULTRY INSTRUCTION."[29]

Most notably, Philo used the institute to offer formal resident and correspondence classes on the Philo system of poultry keeping. Students could learn to make Philo coops in the woodworking shop, do research in the library or take classes in the auditorium or classroom. The Philo system was designed to be used by backyard farmers, so the classes provided the information that amateur poultry raisers needed to get started.

Philo advertised the institute and his system widely, claiming that a forty-square-foot city lot could yield $1,500 a year in poultry profits. The efforts paid off, and he got the attention of both customers and poultry professionals. Testimonials show that the system was widely adopted, but some people had trouble keeping up with the strict schedules and guidelines. The strange system opened Philo up to criticism. Professor John F. Graham of the Amherst Agricultural College said that Philo was a liar and that he "fishes for suckers and he gets them."[30] The *Pacific Coast Fancier's Monthly* claimed that Philo's book was not worth the one-dollar purchase price, claiming it was nothing more than a get-rich-quick scheme that would only serve to discourage potential poultry farmers.[31]

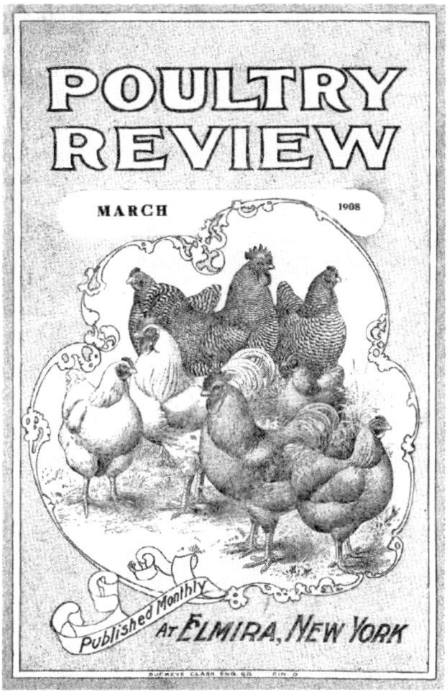

Cover of the March 1908 issue of the *Poultry Review*, published by Philo.

Despite his success selling his system, Philo soon became entangled in drama within his own company. Philo's children, Ernest and Ruth, kicked their father out of the company in 1917 because they disagreed about the use of the property. Philo moved to Florida with the goal of setting up a utopian poultry community on the nearly thirty thousand acres of property he owned. He remained in the poultry business, advertising what he called the "New Philo Way." He died in Pennsylvania in 1937.

While his Philo Institute building still stands, his system and its contributions to poultry science have been largely forgotten. In 1919, Charles Weeks wrote in the *American Poultry Journal* that Philo had "startled the world by a new and unheard of system of keeping poultry in small pens without outside runs." The system, popular with laymen but derided by professionals, ultimately failed because it was too labor intensive. Still, Weeks argued that Philo and his work "added to the poultry industry in that they have provoked thought and experimentation along those lines."[32] One can certainly see echoes of Philo's theories in modern factory farming, but Philo himself would have opposed large-scale poultry production. He loved the industry and thought he was making improvements. Philo summed it up best in 1910: "probably if I had given the same time and attention to some other line of business…I would have been better off in this world's goods, but I liked the poultry business, loved the work and simply could not give it up."[33]

4

THE HUNGERFORD BROTHERS

Daniel and Floyd Hungerford longed for a future of interstellar travel. While the brothers never made it very far off of this planet, they did leave an indelible mark on Elmira and the aviation and rocketry communities.[34]

Daniel was born in 1886, and Floyd was born in 1888. When the Hungerfords moved to Elmira in 1907, they entered an area in the midst of an aviation revolution. In nearby Hammondsport, New York, aviator Glenn Curtiss worked on early airplanes and made pioneering first flights. But Elmira's experimental aviation history stretched back even further. Matthias C. Arnot and Mansel Taylor both designed flying machines in the late nineteenth century. Later, Elmira would become the "Soaring Capital of the World" for its contributions to gliding history. Steeped in this world of flight, the Hungerfords grew up to launch their own attempts to make it into the sky.

The mechanically inclined Hungerford brothers began working on airplane engines in the late 1900s and early 1910s. They built a small working plane engine in 1909. In 1913, they purchased a Bleriot monoplane with Elmiran Stanley Kosmicki. The brothers wanted to use the plane to experiment with a new type of gasoline motor they had invented that they thought was more efficient than any previously used.[35] In May 1914, Daniel Hungerford announced that the plane and engine were almost ready for test flights. He drove the plane around open fields, testing the engine, but he had not yet left the ground. He promised that the plane would be

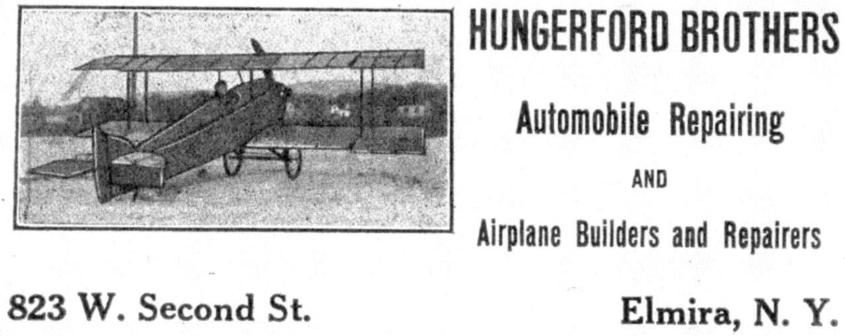

Advertisement for the Hungerford Brothers' automobile and airplane company from the 1921 *Elmira City Directory*.

flown around the city that summer and that the brothers would offer public demonstrations.[36] Over the next few years, the Hungerfords added to their airplane collection. In 1917, the brothers and Kosmicki purchased a plane that could carry passengers.[37]

In 1921, the Hungerfords and their associates formed the Elmira Aeroplane Exhibition Corporation, a multipurpose company that encompassed airplane rides, manufacture, repair and more. The Hungerfords' efforts gained them increasing recognition. The National Aeronautic Association of the United States appointed Daniel to organize an Elmira chapter of the organization, to work with "all boys and girls seventeen years or more of age who wish to take a course in learning how to fly."[38]

Daniel Hungerford worked with local youth to interest them in and educate them about aviation. In 1924, he worked with Elmira Community Service to run a model airplane and kite construction and flying contest for local children.[39] He worked with city playground supervisors to teach them how to build model airplanes, and he encouraged their charges to enter the National Model Airplane Contest.[40] He also taught some of the Elmira Community Service boys how to repair actual planes.[41]

The Hungerfords, inspired by international rocketry experiments in the late 1920s, decided to do their own work in that field. For most people in the 1920s, the idea of interplanetary travel was a joke or fodder for science fiction. Philip Francis Nowlan's 1928 novella *Armageddon 2419 A.D.* introduced Americans to the character Buck Rogers. This in turn inspired the popular *Buck Rogers in the 25th Century A.D.* comic strip in 1929 and radio

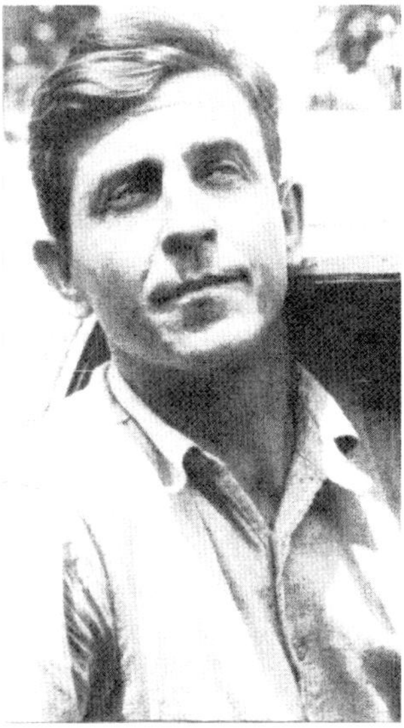

Daniel Hungerford.

show in 1932. Buck Rogers films followed in the 1930s. Elmirans would have been familiar with rockets in fiction, but they would not have expected to see a rocket car on the streets of their city.

Ultimately, Daniel and Floyd's 1929 foray into rocketry was terrestrial, rather than interplanetary. Working with John Albee and J. Emory Botsford, they built a rocket car on the chassis of a 1921 Chevrolet. The body of the car was made from cardboard and linoleum so that the driver could make a quick exit by kicking out the sides if necessary. The car had a conventional gasoline engine in addition to a rocket tube. Once the car got underway using the regular engine, the driver could activate the rocket engine, at which time the vehicle could reach speeds of seventy miles per hour and shoot a flame twenty feet long from the back. The car only went two miles for each gallon of gas. The completed Hungerford rocket car was named "Shirley Lois, Moon Girl," after Daniel's young daughter. Signaling the brothers' greater ambitions, "Hungerford Rockets, Solar & Interstellar" was emblazoned on the car.

The brothers first tested their invention on November 2, 1929, running it only on the gasoline engine. Chemung County officially licensed the car in 1931, allowing it to be legally driven on the streets.[42] The rocket car then became a fixture at fairs and other events, where the brothers would explain rocketry to interested crowds and give demonstrations. A report on one community event stated, "Hungerford's rocket ship, for solar and interplanetary trips, is unique."[43] Organizers of the Century of Progress in Chicago in 1933 and the New York World's Fair in 1939 were not as impressed with the invention, however; both exhibitions refused to display the car. In 1934, the Hungerfords' rocket car was mentioned on the Buck Rogers radio show. The brothers' experiments with rocket power were not limited to their car: they also created a rocket-powered soldering iron and devised plans for a rocket-powered lawn mower, which never came to fruition.

The rocket car met mixed local response, with many Elmirans not understanding why one would invest time and money in such an endeavor.

In fact, the Hungerfords' political views may have been another factor in the public response to their invention. While they were doing their mechanical work, the brothers were also active in the Socialist Party. Each ran for a variety of local offices, but as third-party candidates from a party viewed by many with suspicion and fear, neither was ever elected. Daniel also made headlines when he protested the demolition of Elmira's Langdon Mansion in 1939. The Langdon home belonged to Mark Twain's in-laws and was where Twain and Olivia Langdon were married. His efforts failed, however, and the building was torn down.

The Hungerfords and collaborators modified the rocket car in the decades after its invention. They stopped displaying it in the mid-1930s. The brothers became increasingly reclusive. Daniel's marriage ended, and the brothers once again shared a house. Floyd died in 1963. Ralph Hodge and Keith Martin convinced Daniel to let them take the rocket car to Cohoes, New York, where Hodge repaired the machine and again exhibited it. In 1966, the City of Elmira evicted Daniel from his home for failing to pay his taxes. The house was torn down. He died on April 10, 1967. The rocket car was donated to the New York State Museum in Albany in 1992.

PART II

CRAZY CRIMES

From committing assault and murder to engaging in fraud and sex trafficking, some Elmirans made their names in less than reputable ways. While crime has always occurred in Elmira, as in all other cities, the instances in this chapter made headlines for their uniqueness. In some cases, the perpetrator was someone of note; in other cases, the victim was a high-profile figure. The outrageous nature of these crimes made them fodder for local and, in some cases, national gossip.

5

POLITICAL ASSAULTS

On the morning of October 20, 1884, New York governor Grover Cleveland walked through the streets of Albany, following his regular route to the executive chamber in the state capitol building. This, however, was not a regular morning. At the intersection of Lancaster and Eagle Streets, a man emerged and attacked Cleveland. The assailant was Samuel T. Boom, a twenty-eight-year-old machinist from Elmira.

Boom threw two punches at Cleveland, which the governor deflected. At some point during this struggle, Cleveland got a minor cut behind his ear. When his first method of attack failed, Boom retreated and found a paving stone. His attempt to throw the stone at the governor, however, was thwarted, and he was restrained by Dr. George H. Houghton, a bystander. Boom yelled that the governor was killing his wife and that he was seeking revenge. Denied the opportunity for further attack, Boom fled to his nearby boardinghouse.

Boom was arrested shortly after. Cleveland, relatively unscathed, continued with his usual business and morning meetings. Neither the governor nor reporters considered Boom an actual threat to anyone. Boom was reportedly "a small, delicate man" who "looks wild but talks rationally."[44]

When Boom did talk, however rationally, he told a strange tale to explain his motive for the attack. A few weeks prior, Governor Cleveland had visited Elmira on business. While in the city, he met Boom's wife, who asked Cleveland to pardon her brother. Mrs. Boom's brother was in the Auburn Prison for shooting at some boys. Cleveland promised to review the case, which he did when he returned to Albany. He consulted with the district attorney, who advised Cleveland not to issue a pardon in this case. But Cleveland took a while longer to issue his decision, citing the need to examine the large number of pardon requests on his desk in the order in which they were received. In the meantime, the Booms came to Albany to follow up on their request. Mr. Boom met with Cleveland, who informed him that while he had yet to make an official decision on the case, the district attorney and Elmira law enforcement opposed the pardon. Distressed by the news, Boom threatened to "slap his chops" and vowed to remain in Albany until the pardon was granted.

Still without a satisfactory answer days later, Mrs. Boom went to the see the governor. She was so upset that she had to be forcibly removed from the capitol building. In the struggle, her arm was bruised. Mr. Boom blamed Cleveland personally for her injury. Boom reported that his wife's health had been failing due to the stress of her brother's case and that the whole ordeal was killing her.

At this point, Boom decided that more desperate measures were necessary. For days after his wife's incident at the capitol, Boom stalked Cleveland, learning his daily schedule. Boom's actions were not too covert, however, as he was spotted several times by the governor and his staff. He also was said to have threatened the governor's life, saying that he would shoot Cleveland if only he had a gun. Warned that Boom might pose a threat, the governor nevertheless deemed him "harmless."[45]

After the failed attack, Boom pled not guilty. During his arraignment, he claimed that his wife's hysteria had progressed to the point where she was unconscious. Boom was ultimately released without punishment. The sad finale to the story, however, was that a pardon would not have helped Mrs. Boom's brother. While the whole ordeal had been unfolding in Albany, prison officials deemed her brother insane and transferred him from general population to the insane ward.

Sixteen years later, on October 29, 1900, New York governor Theodore Roosevelt was assaulted in Elmira. He was touring the country as the vice presidential running mate for incumbent president William McKinley's reelection campaign. Roosevelt undertook an unusually ambitious touring schedule; the same day he was in Elmira, he had already visited Cortland, Ithaca and Van Etten. In many towns and cities, he was met with violence and protest, as the contentious campaign pitted McKinley's Republican supporters against those of Democrat William Jennings Bryan. In the three months before the election, he faced significant mobs and other disturbances in Colorado, Indiana, Ohio and other states.[46] The Elmira incident was one of many acts of violence on the trail.

In Elmira, an estimated twenty thousand people descended on the city for his planned events. A centerpiece of his visit was a parade that featured between five hundred and one thousand Rough Rider supporters. The parade, which began at 7:00 p.m., led to his first speaking engagement at a local theater. Roosevelt and Jacob Sloat Fassett, an Elmiran and former senator, rode in a carriage not far behind the mounted riders.

Riding behind the Rough Riders was a disheveled man on a donkey. The rider held a sign reading "Alone in Cuba," the title that humorist Finley Peter Dunne suggested Roosevelt should have used for his best-selling memoir *The Rough Riders*, because of his tendency to highlight his personal contributions in the war. This critic of Roosevelt was not a sanctioned part of the parade, and his appearance seemed to inspire Bryanists and other men to interrupt the parade and the governor's passage. A mob of about fifty men started to surround the governor's carriage.

The men were armed with vegetables and other projectiles. Ironically, it seems that they got some of their ammunition from the parade itself. The parade featured a "prosperity wagon," which held a large metal pail of food items that were tossed into the crowd. This was a literal interpretation of McKinley's "Full Dinner Pail" campaign slogan. Some in the crowd began to throw the vegetables back.[47] As Roosevelt's carriage turned from Water Street onto Main Street and then reached the Church Street intersection, the mob grew to about three hundred people and became increasingly unruly. People threw rocks, sticks and whatever else they could. Eventually, some of the Rough Riders up ahead were able to drop back and escort the carriage to safety.

There were other eruptions of violence throughout the day. An incident happened on Lake Street, where uniformed Republican supporters from Corning with large McKinley banners were attacked by stone-throwing boys. A second fight broke out later, at the corner of Water Street and Railroad Avenue. An officer fired his gun into the air to disperse the crowd. A band drum major from Waverly only lost one beat when someone tried to grab his sheet music during the parade and he hit the man in the hand with his stick.[48] One member of a McKinley supporters' group from Corning was sent to the hospital with a nonserious back injury.

In Corning the next day, Roosevelt spoke briefly about the Elmira incident, decrying the violence of the Bryan supporters. He said:

> *I think that sooner or later our opponents will grow to understand that mob violence is not the way to try to keep Republicans back.... Your fellow townsmen who have come back from Elmira to-day were not merely booted, but they were maltreated scandalously by a mob which wished to break up the meeting and procession last night.*[49]

He also noted, "Now is the time to stamp out Bryanism....The affair at Elmira last night cast shame upon the country where the right of free speech should be observed."[50]

Others echoed Roosevelt's disgust for the tactics of the mobs. The *Port Jervis Tri-States Union*, in a long anti-Bryan screed, declared, "Down with Elmira thuggism." The newspaper also accused the Elmira police officers of being Bryan supporters, looking on passively while the mob attacked and allowing the Bryanists' "loaferism, and hoodlumism and free riot."[51] C.A. Pulford, chairman of the Chemung County Republican Committee, wrote a letter to the *New York Daily Tribune* to draw attention to the violence. The newspaper printed a photograph of the stick, turnip and shoe recovered from Roosevelt's carriage.[52] Chemung County Democratic chairman George M. Robinson made a statement in an attempt to distance the philosophy of his party from the actions of the mobs. He said, "We regret Governor Roosevelt should have met with such a reception in the streets of our city."[53] The *New York Times* called it "The Elmira Disturbance," saying that the fights were more "prolonged, savage, vindictive, and bloody" than those in the Wild West.[54]

In the aftermath, harsh criticism fell on the Elmira police. There was a general increase in crime during Roosevelt's visit, with a reported theft of thirteen pocketbooks and various instances of drunkenness during his speeches. Special police officers had been stationed around the parade route, but some witnesses said that they did little to help. Opening an investigation into the matter, police commissioner Henry L. Armstrong said, "Any officer on the police forces who was negligent in his duty last night will get it in the neck."[55]

Chief of Police Frank Cassada released a statement saying that he had been unaware that Roosevelt was even going to be participating in the parade. He thought that the governor would instead be watching the procession from the safety of the Hotel Rathbun. Cassada said, " I regret the affair as much as any one."[56] On November 1, the Elmira police commissioners offered a twenty-five-dollar reward to anyone who could provide information that would lead to the conviction of any persons involved in the assault, saying, "there is no excuse for the affair."[57] That evening, the board of police commissioners met for four hours, examining the incident and evidence. About thirty witnesses had already been interviewed, and fifty more were to be interviewed soon. Some witnesses blamed the Corning Roosevelt supporters for starting some of the violence. Allegedly, a Corning Rough Rider hit another man with a torch, which inspired a round of rock throwing.[58]

Police commissioner Armstrong said the commissioners determined that the incident was "a spontaneous outburst on the part of boys, young lads and hoodlums, who were following up a man grotesquely dressed and riding a donkey." He also claimed that the participants were only boys, none more than seventeen years old. Ultimately, the findings were in part a product of political motivation. Armstrong said, "I am coming out flat-footed in this affair. I am doing so merely to remove a blot and stain from the fair name of Proud Elmira, and I am not willing to allow any wrong impression to go abroad which will hurt Elmira's fair name."[59] And with that, the "Elmira Disturbance" was written off as an instance of youthful indiscretion.

6

THE GREAT FEMALE CRIME SPREE

In 1890, Elmira was rocked by three high-profile instances of crimes committed by women. While female-driven crime was not uncommon, Ella White, Mary Eilenberger and Mary Fairman found special infamy for the seriousness of their alleged offenses. The forger, murderer and human trafficker, respectively, captivated people in Elmira and across the country.

Until April 1889, Elmirans knew Ella White as a pretty local music teacher. After that, her name became synonymous with forgery, gambling and a brazen prison break. Her actions set off a chain of events that resonated for years and that is still shrouded in mystery.

White was known around the city for her expensive taste. Even while teaching music lessons, she wore silks and furs and adorned herself with diamonds and expensive jewelry. Such finery, above her socioeconomic status, raised suspicion. Soon, the need to maintain her lavish lifestyle caused White to make risky, even illegal, financial decisions.

She claimed that her money was in mining stocks and that she sometimes needed loans to pay her bills until her stocks paid out. White took chattel mortgages on her clothing and jewels for $1,050. She also began asking friends and acquaintances for personal loans. She borrowed large amounts of money from some but also accepted smaller amounts from poorer women. As her debts accumulated, the patience of her creditors wore thin. When she failed to repay one man $500, he took her seal skin coat and diamonds as payment. All the while, White claimed she would repay her creditors when her stock fortunes changed.

White's stocks never made her any money. In all likelihood, this is because she did not actually have any stocks. Her supposed agent for the mining stocks denied that she had ever worked with him or purchased stocks through his business. She also claimed to have $8,000 worth of stocks in a Massachusetts silk mill. This was also untrue. As her desperation grew, White began forging bank notes under the name "Mrs. Brown."[60]

Her continued deception hid a dark financial secret: she had lost a lot of money in a local bucket shop. Bucket shops were places where people would speculate and bet on the price of stocks without actually purchasing any shares. She gambled in the bucket shop at 156 Baldwin Street, owned by A.C. Wheeler. He lived in the same boardinghouse as White. As the press explained, she "dabbled heavily in stocks and lost."[61]

After receiving complaints, the police seized a piano for which she had received a $200 chattel mortgage. She did not actually own the piano, however; she rented it from piano manufacturer Jacob Greener. When the news of her scandal broke in early April, White fled to her parents' home in Susquehanna, Pennsylvania. When reporters found her there, she claimed that she would be able to pay back all of her debts. She also insisted that she had never gambled. As the investigation intensified, White went to Chicago. She was arrested there on December 4, 1889, and brought back to Elmira. However, the drama was just beginning.

On January 6, 1890, White broke out of the Chemung County Jail. Immediate searches for the fugitive failed, and the jail's turnkey, Isaac Garrabrant, was fired. No one could figure out how she had done it. The Chemung County sheriff offered a $400 reward for her capture.

In the days after her escape, the press joked about the incident. The *Owego Record* quipped, "That the explanatory word, 'financier,' attached to the name of Ella White, if spelled, 'find-an'-see her' would better express what the officials would like to do."[62] The *Elmira Telegram* speculated on how White had escaped. The newspaper's illustrator drew four possible scenarios: shimmying down a water pipe, dressing in a disguise, fleeing on a white horse and flying off on a broom.[63] Others said the "ruddy-cheeked, buxom-formed, auburn haired female" was in a Montreal convent.[64]

The police followed more plausible leads, however. Sheriff Frank Cassada got a tip that she had taken the Northern Central train to Watkins Glen, where she stayed overnight at the Jefferson House. He determined that the "Mrs. Kate Smith" who had stayed there and signed the ledger was White. He thought she might have been on her way to Canada. If she was, he was confident she would be captured soon.[65] The disgraced Isaac Garrabrant claimed that a veiled woman showed up at his house and told his wife to send her husband to an address on Madison Avenue. When Garrabrant and Officer Michael Leydon arrived, the woman who opened the door said the person who called for Garrabrant was no longer there. Garrabrant speculated that White had called for him, hoping that he would be so angry about his dismissal that he would help her in a scheme.[66]

Despite her continued absence, White was indicted for her jailbreak. In February 1891, a female forger in Ohio gave the name "Ella White" when arrested. The woman turned out to be Helen Rogers, not White, and the *Elmira Telegram* opined, "Her crimes are enough without stealing the strawberry blond livery of Elmira's own financier, Ella, to serve the devil in."[67] In July 1891, White was rumored to be in Newburgh, New York, but that also turned out to be untrue.

In May 1892, police in Chicago arrested Etta Robinson when an Elmira visitor to the city insisted that Robinson was White. Again, the woman was not White.[68] As the details of the mistaken arrest of innocent Chicagoan Robinson came out in the local press, the *Elmira Daily Gazette and Free Press* wrote, "The name of Ella White savours of the ridiculous....Any mention of the name of Ella White is just now a signal for hilarity and smiles."[69]

White was never caught. As the years passed, she was occasionally mentioned in the news. In 1899, people joked that she had gone to Cuba dressed as a man and fought in the Spanish-American War.[70] Other jailbreaks were compared to White's historic escape. One of the last rumors about her whereabouts was that she was running a poultry farm outside Chicago.

Just days after Ella White's jailbreak, Mary Eilenberger rose to infamy. On January 10, 1890, she shot and killed William Edwards at her home at 502 East Church Street. Eilenberger and Williams had had a long-running affair, and on the day of the shooting, the pair had an intense domestic dispute. Edwards pulled out a gun.

When police came to Eilenberger's home on January 10, they found her sobbing. In the hall nearby, Edwards's body lay in a pool of blood on the floor. He had been shot in the back of the head. The police arrested Eilenberger for murder. The incident and ensuing trial divided the public into supporters who viewed Eilenberger as a victim who acted in self-defense and those who saw her as a cold-blooded murderess.

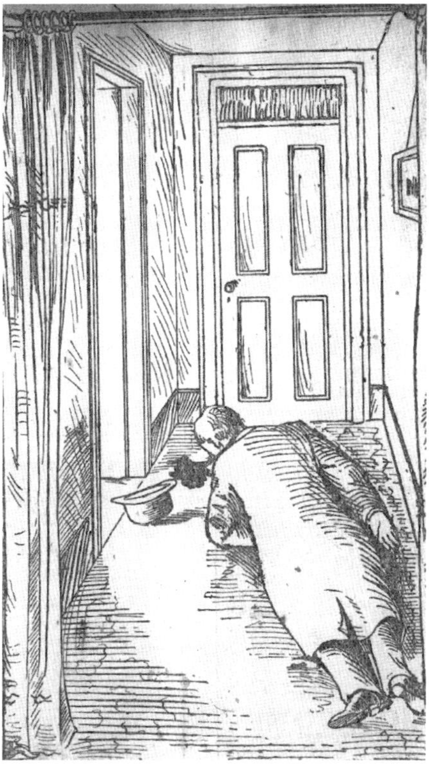

A drawing of the crime scene showing William Edwards's body in the hallway of Mary Eilenberger's home.

Eilenberger and Edwards, both in their mid- to late forties, had maintained their relationship despite the fact that both were married to other people. Reportedley, Eilenberger had lived apart from her husband and children for seven years, and Edwards had a wife and young child. Edwards was a politician, farmer, gambler and con man from nearby Van Etten. They couple had a contentious relationship. In 1888, Edwards had accused Eilenberger of arson when her house burned down, but she was not indicted. He allegedly blackmailed her into loaning him thousands of dollars.

She told the police that Edwards had come to her house looking for money and they began to fight. The pair reportedly had gambling debts.[71] Edwards got a gun from the bedroom, and the two began struggling for the weapon. Eilenberger claimed that the gun accidentally fired in the fight, killing Edwards.[72] Chief of Police Levi Little examined the body at the scene and considered the entry wound on the back of Edwards's head suspicious. He conferred with the coroner, and he agreed that it was likely murder.[73]

On January 15, 1890, the Chemung County grand jury indicted Eilenberger for murder in the first degree. The key argument leading to her indictment posited that if the gun accidentally discharged, Edwards would not have been hit in the back of the head. The public was divided on this fact. Many agreed with the prosecution, seeing the bullet's entry as proof of her guilt. Others, however, argued that Edwards could have accidentally shot himself in the back of the head during the struggle if he was holding the gun above and behind his head to keep it away from Eilenberger. In that scenario, the barrel could have been pointed toward him.[74] Eilenberger was kept in jail until her trial, scheduled to start later that year. She reportedly suffered from "nervous prostration" while awaiting her trial.[75] Finally, on October 18, the jury was set, and the trial began.

The salacious trial was followed closely in the press. Eilenberger's lawyers argued that the shooting was self-defense and justifiable. According to testimony, Edwards had been stealing money from Eilenberger during their relationship, having already claimed over $8,000 of her money. On the day of Edwards's death, he had tried to take even more from her pocketbook.

The defense, led by lawyer Jacob Schwartz, argued that Eilenberger was a battered woman. Her lawyers presented evidence to support her claims that Edwards had abused her for years. He had threatened her with a gun before and committed other acts of violence against her. The testimony was reportedly so graphic that Edwards's widow and child left the courtroom.[76]

Eilenberger's lawyers also tried to prove that Edwards could have accidentally shot himself in the struggle. His skull was entered as evidence. Dr. H.D. Pratt, called as a defense witness, testified that it was possible. He demonstrated the position that Edwards's arm would have had to be in for the bullet to enter at the angle it did. Dr. William C. Wey and Dr. Henry Flood shared similar findings. Other character witnesses were called to defend her reputation. In his closing statement, Schwartz described the emotional state of his client leading up to the shooting: "The woman is under the complete subjection of this man's power. He has gained control of her, body and soul, and now attempts to absorb her means.…The time had come when he had sucked the juice from the orange and was about to throw away the peel."[77]

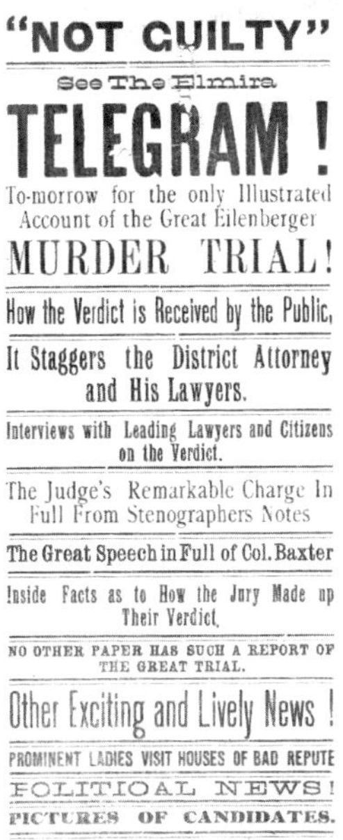

"NOT GUILTY"

See The Elmira

TELEGRAM !

To-morrow for the only Illustrated Account of the Great Eilenberger

MURDER TRIAL!

How the Verdict is Received by the Public,

It Staggers the District Attorney and His Lawyers.

Interviews with Leading Lawyers and Citizens on the Verdict.

The Judge's Remarkable Charge In Full From Stenographers Notes

The Great Speech in Full of Col. Baxter

Inside Facts as to How the Jury Made up Their Verdict.

NO OTHER PAPER HAS SUCH A REPORT OF THE GREAT TRIAL.

Other Exciting and Lively News !

PROMINENT LADIES VISIT HOUSES OF BAD REPUTE

POLITICAL NEWS!

PICTURES OF CANDIDATES.

St. Patrick's New Church Illustration,

Handbill produced by the *Elmira Telegram* announcing the results of the Eilenberger murder trial.

On October 18, 1890, the jury found Eilenberger not guilty of murder. The verdict shocked many in the community who had assumed her guilt. A writer at the *Elmira Telegram*, not disguising his bias, wrote, "the great Eilenberger murder trial was a thing of the past, only to remain indelibly fixed in the minds of all decent people as a travesty on justice."[78] Others took a different view of the verdict. Reverend Thomas K. Beecher wrote an article in the *Elmira Daily Advertiser*, opining, "At this present, I see no objection to the plan, that all mistresses, courtezans and common prostitutes sleep henceforth with revolvers under their pillows, and use them at will upon any and every male visitor as he goes out the door. I do not see any damage would accrue to society thereby." The local press was outraged over the suggestion that adulterers deserved to be shot. Beecher later attempted to explain his position, but he did not apologize.[79]

Although Eilenberger was cleared of all wrongdoing in the case, the rest of her life was not without more controversy. The trial bankrupted her, and she was forced to move to Waverly, New York, to live with her children. On November 17, 1891, her son Bennie Watts was arrested in Waverly for intoxication and assaulting her and his sister.[80] By 1892, she was seriously ill. In December of that year, she wrote a letter again proclaiming her innocence in the case. She gave it to her lawyer so that her side of the story could be told if she died soon.[81]

Eilenberger died of consumption on August 19, 1893, just weeks after her daughter met the same fate. Her obituary noted that her "fifty-two years of life had been crowded with experiences more exciting and disheartening than fall to the lot of the average man or woman." The *Elmira Telegram*, still convinced of her guilt, opined, "The sad ending of this woman's life teaches a moral so plain that any one familiar with her career can readily see it."[82]

In early 1890, Elmirans witnessed the trial of Mary Fairman, whom the Elmira papers called "the most depraved woman ever allowed in this city." Her sullied reputation was well known and reported on in large Brooklyn newspapers and the *New York Times.* Over a period of six years, from 1885 to 1891, Fairman was involved in a series of scandals, each more salacious than the next. Among other alleged crimes, she was accused of trafficking young girls out of Brooklyn and selling them into Elmira's sex industry.

Mary Fairman and her husband, Jared, owned a dry goods store in Elmira from the 1880s into the early 1890s. In popular local historical memory, this era was the height of economic and social life in Elmira, an industrial and cultural hub that was frequented by celebrities such as Mark Twain. Yet, there was another side to the city that was enabled by this prosperity. Prostitution flourished and went relatively unchecked. The rise of Elmira's sex industry was spurred by two major factors: the Civil War and railroads.

During the war, Elmira was established as a military rendezvous point and the site of a Confederate prisoner-of-war camp. As a result, thousands of young men flooded the area, increasing not only the population of the city but also the demand for prostitution. Elmira was an important railroad stop by the 1850s; by the turn of the twentieth century, dozens of passenger trains passed through the city daily. Saloons, hotels, brothels and gambling houses sprang up on Railroad Avenue, Water Street and other streets surrounding the railroad lines in order to service travelers and railroad workers. The frequency of passenger trains allowed young girls to easily, and relatively cheaply, come to the city to find work. Many of these girls found work as domestics or in other fields, but others became prostitutes.

It was in this social climate that Mary Fairman allegedly brought at least four girls from Brooklyn to Elmira and was arrested for trying to sell a local girl to a brothel. The Fairmans lived in Brooklyn in the late 1870s, and during that time, Mary Fairman befriended several girls and mothers. After the Fairmans moved back to Elmira, Fairman began using her Brooklyn connections to bring girls to her Elmira shop. At some point in 1885, Fairman convinced sisters Josephine and Flora Caluette to come to Elmira. By the winter of 1885, sixteen-year-old Flora had run away from the Fairmans. Her younger sister, Josie, who was fourteen years old, ran away the following spring. At the time, the Caluette sisters' experience went unnoticed by the press. Later articles, however, revealed that the girls had become well-known local "disorderly persons," or prostitutes. In fact, the Fairmans' influence over the Caluette girls came to light only when another sixteen-year-old, Ada Hull, went to the police after her encounter with the Fairmans.

Brooklyn resident Ada Hull came to Elmira with Mary Fairman on June 4, 1886, and by the end of that month, she was back home. Hull's scandalous tale of her time with the Fairmans filled the Brooklyn newspapers. According to Hull, Fairman had promised her an education, fine clothing and an introduction to a wealthy young man. Hull's mother was reluctant to let her daughter go, but she was ultimately convinced by Fairman.

However, when Hull arrived in Elmira, she did not receive the treatment she had expected. She claimed that the Fairmans forced her to work in their store and that they abused her. Hull also made allegations of sexual impropriety against the Fairmans. She claimed that many young men frequented the store and that Mary Fairman forced her to spend time with them. Hull alleged that Jared Fairman "insulted" her by grabbing, kissing and hugging her without her consent. She also said that he showed her "immoral pictures." During Hull's brief tenure at the store, Mary Fairman rehired Flora Caluette. Fairman told Hull that having pretty girls in the store drew in male customers. Hull insinuated that Flora Caluette met the men outside the store as well but insisted that she was not the "same sort of girl."[83]

On June 23, Ada Hull went to Elmira chief of police Levi Little for help. Hull told the police and, in turn, the press, that she had told the Fairmans that she wanted to leave and that, when they denied her request, she threatened to commit suicide. Mary Fairman told Hull that she would have her arrested, so Hull ran away with the help of the Caluette girls. After hiding in a cemetery, she went to the police station and was sent back to Brooklyn.[84]

After Hull's story broke in the news, Mary Fairman pled her case to the Brooklyn newspapers. She claimed that she never wanted to take Hull to Elmira but did so only at the girl's mother's insistence. Hull, Fairman stated, was wild and was spending time with disreputable people. After Hull ran away, the Fairmans contacted the police, who initially refused to look for the girl. Despite Mary's account, the primary narrative reported in the newspapers was unflattering to the Fairmans. In response, Mary Fairman sued the *New York Morning Journal* for $10,000 for libel. This suit set the stage for Mary Fairman's future encounters with the law.

About two weeks after Ada Hull's return to Brooklyn, the Fairmans were back in the press, regarding the disappearance of another Brooklyn girl. On July 7, 1886, news broke that thirteen-year-old Emily Duryea had eloped to Elmira with seventeen-year-old Alfred Nichols. Duryea, whose mother had died and whose father was unreliable, had been living with Phoebe Hull, the mother of Ada Hull. Nichols and Duryea, traveling by train, became separated at Kingston, New York. The pair ran out of money, so Nichols went on to Elmira without her by stowing away on freight trains. When he reached Elmira, he implored Mary Fairman to send Duryea money, and she obliged.[85]

When Duryea arrived in Elmira, she announced that she never had any intention of marrying Nichols. Instead, Nichols was just trying to prevent Duryea from being put in an institution. Mary Fairman also claimed pity as a reason for helping Duryea. However, Fairman had another motive: she wanted Duryea, an acquaintance of Ada Hull, to be a witness for her in her libel suit.

As with Hull, the arrangement Duryea had with the Fairmans did not last long. In early September 1886, Duryea fled the Fairmans' store through a window and rode a tin peddler's wagon to the train depot to board a train back to Brooklyn. She allegedly grew tired of work in the Fairmans' store and was upset that she had not received the dresses and other fineries she had been promised. By September 8, she was back home.

After Duryea's flight, the Elmira papers speculated that perhaps now Mary Fairman would stop her "benefactress business" with the Brooklyn girls. Aside from an incident in 1888 when her dog was accused of mauling a neighbor's dog to death, it appears that Fairman managed to stay out of the gossip columns for several years. However, that changed in dramatic fashion in late 1889. On October 18, an Elmira woman, Mattie Barber, was arrested for trying to sell twelve-year-old Emma Miller to a well-known brothel on West Water Street. Miller, from Elmira, was the daughter of a drunkard father and an absent mother and was quickly becoming notorious for misbehavior. Barber had contacted Carrie Moore, madam of the "Bay Window resort," about the girl coming to work for Moore. Barber told Moore that the girl was sixteen years old, but Moore knew something was wrong and contacted the police. When Barber came to Moore's establishment to deliver Miller, the police were waiting. Both Barber and Miller were arrested in the sting operation.

When Miller and Barber were brought to the police station, both claimed that Mary Fairman was the mastermind behind the entire plot. According to Barber, Fairman was afraid that Miller, who had spent time at the Fairmans' home, would testify in the libel trial that Fairman was running a disorderly house. To prevent this, Fairman devised a plan to get Miller to her house by saying that the girl's estranged mother wanted to meet her there. When Miller arrived, Fairman instead tried to convince her not only to testify for her in the libel case but also to defame the men who worked for the *Journal*. When Miller refused, Fairman hatched a plan with Barber to discredit the girl so that she would not be a reliable witness for the newspaper. To do so, she offered Barber $1,000 (of the money she hoped to win in the suit) to bring the girl to a house of prostitution. When Miller corroborated the story, the police arrested Fairman for abduction.

The details of the case were exposed over the next few months at Barber's and Fairman's trials. Ultimately, Barber pled guilty to abduction and was sentenced to pay a fine of $175 or to spend 175 days in jail; she chose to serve her term.[86] Mary Fairman was found not guilty on March 28, 1890.[87]

Fairman's libel suit was yet to be decided. The trial took place in January 1891 and proved sensational in the local press. The *Elmira Telegram* printed a transcript of the trial, revealing that Fairman gave conflicting testimony about details of her personal life. Among the revelations in the transcript were that she had been suspected of committing arson in Pennsylvania and that she had sued a Brooklyn man for slander for saying she was an immoral woman.[88] When the trial concluded on January 18, Fairman lost her libel suit.

After 1891, the Fairmans disappear from Elmira city directories and censuses. They first moved to Corning and then, by 1905, were living in Buffalo. After they left Elmira, the Fairmans seem to have stayed out of the press.

About twenty years after the Fairman incidents, a "white slavery" panic swept the nation. Lawmakers, the press and reform groups shared sensationalized stories of young white girls being sold into the sex trade. Historians now recognize that this phenomenon was rooted more in hysteria than in actual fact. Cases like those of Mary Fairman, the Brooklyn girls and Emma Miller show how complicated sex trafficking and prostitution were in the late nineteenth and early twentieth centuries. Despite the accusations leveled against her, Mary Fairman was never convicted of a crime. She may have never intended to run an immoral house or to bring girls into prostitution. Still, her actions are reflective of how many young women became prostitutes in Elmira. From the few accounts available of prostitutes' individual histories, we know that many came from broken families and were convinced by someone to come to the city.

Elmira never established a legal red-light district, but for decades, prostitution went relatively unchecked. As Mary Fairman's story illustrates, punishments were often lenient or nonexistent, and there was cooperation between madams and the police. While Fairman's story was more publicized than others, it was not atypical for Elmira and other cities.

7

LEW GILMORE VS. ANTHONY COMSTOCK

Lewis C. Gilmore was an affable fixture of the local social scene. Known for his kindness and quirks, "Lew" was successful in his various business endeavors. He was an innovator in local advertising, gaining popularity for his attention-grabbing poems and slogans. Ironically, it was some of his creative advertisements that landed him in serious trouble with moral crusader Anthony Comstock.

Born in Philadelphia in the 1850s, Gilmore moved with his family to Schuyler County, New York. When he was seventeen, he went to Elmira to live with his older brother Billy and found work caring for horses for local men. He soon found a job in a general store, which led to employment as a traveling salesman in the shipping department of Simons, Sayles & Company. In 1877, he married Clementine McCann.

As his family expanded, so did Gilmore's business acumen. He purchased property at the corner of High and East Second Streets and built a grocery store, which he ran until 1887. Then he opened Gilmore's Great Grocery on State Street. He did good business and earned a positive reputation for gestures like giving the local newsboys a bushel of candy for Christmas in 1891.[89] He ran Gilmore's Great Grocery until 1892, when he sold it, left the grocery business and opened a saloon.

The Blue Front saloon, at 146 East Water Street, was as offbeat as its owner. Gilmore painted the entire interior blue, even the picture frames, and he placed a blue hogshead outside. The floor was strewn with eggshells, a product of the free hard-boiled eggs that Gilmore offered with beer purchases.

He made no effort to remove them, instead embracing the crunchy shells as a defining characteristic of his establishment.

In addition to beer and eggs, Gilmore's Blue Front provided another product: bawdy cards. The cards featured poems that were reportedly "exceedingly suggestive in some instances and positively indecent in others."[90] Patrons of the Blue Front could purchase the cards at the bar, or people could write to Gilmore requesting the naughty poems. Gilmore did swift business in this trade, selling thousands of cards across the country.

Soon, however, his illicit card empire drew unwanted attention. Offended people wrote letters to Anthony Comstock, asking him to intervene. Comstock, a postal inspector, created the New York Society for the Suppression of Vice in 1873 with the mission of destroying immorality. When Congress passed the Comstock Law that year, it became illegal to send obscene materials through the mail. Comstock personally participated in the investigation and arrest of suspected producers and distributors of pornography and obscenity, including Lew Gilmore.

On September 9, 1893, Comstock, using the pseudonym A. Bauer, wrote a letter to Gilmore. Gilmore responded and sent eleven of his cards on September 27. With that evidence in hand, Comstock went to Elmira to investigate further. Comstock, still pretending to be Bauer, went to Gilmore's home with copies of their correspondence, and Gilmore offered to provide him with more cards. Gilmore had been charging three dollars for one thousand cards, but noted that he was having twenty-six thousand more printed soon and would be able to offer them at the discounted price of one dollar per one thousand. Comstock then went to the Blue Front, where he purchased another pack of cards from the bartender, John Curley.

After Comstock purchased the cards from Curley, he brought the evidence to Elmira's chief of police, Levi Little, and obtained a warrant. Little and Comstock returned to the Blue Front and arrested Curley. Gilmore was arrested by a U.S. marshal soon after. Comstock found 17,400 cards and a stack of letters requesting cards. Finding the bill from the printer for the additional 26,000 cards on order, Comstock then arrested Charles and John Harrison, brothers who owned a print shop on Carroll Street.

Public opinion on the case was divided. Fellow bar owners worried that Comstock would also target their own illicit dealings. Reportedly, "a number of saloon-keepers who have kept bare bust pictures on exhibition in their places hastily removed them." Another expressed his disgust about Gilmore's actions: "the idea of a man resorting to such vile tactics to drum up a trade, and to think of a married man with little children, resorting to such a disgraceful business [was] awful, and a disgrace to our city."[91] The *Elmira Daily Gazette and Free Press* stated:

> *The work of Anthony Comstock in this city should be commended by every decent citizen. The cards which have been given away for some time past at the saloon of L.C. Gilmore are indescribably vile. The abatement of this moral nuisance may not be a pleasant task but should be sternly pursued. The filthiness is unspeakable. The suppression of this literature and the punishment of those responsible for it are sanitary proceedings for which the public should be grateful.*[92]

Still others came to Gilmore's defense. An anonymous friend granted an interview with the *Elmira Telegram*, in which he claimed Gilmore was "not exactly in his right mind." He blamed Gilmore's years of hard work in the grocery business for "unbalancing" him and driving him into the saloon business. The friend quoted several of Gilmore's other non-lewd business cards as evidence. They featured self-deprecating poems referencing his failure in business and a meditation on drunkenness. Addressing the card scandal and other puzzling behavior, he concluded, "I say in all charity that Lewis C. Gilmore wasn't just right in his mind when he did the queer and freakish things that I have mentioned."[93]

Gilmore's preliminary court examination began on November 17, 1893. Reportedly, Comstock was considering allowing the local justice system to deal with the case and not bringing it to federal court. That changed, however, when one of Gilmore's lawyers, Colonel Joseph P. Eustace, insulted Comstock on the street. The offended Comstock then decided to pursue the case, focusing even more attention on it to avenge the personal slight.[94]

In late November, Gilmore was indicted by the grand jury for possessing and distributing obscene literature. Bartender John Curley was not indicted, but the Harrison brothers were.[95] Gilmore's trial was scheduled for the beginning of the new session of the United States Court in Albany in January. In the meantime, a group of prominent local men attempted to exert their influence to free Gilmore, arguing that "Lew has always been a pretty decent sort of fellow."[96] They were unsuccessful.

When the new court term opened on January 16, 1894, locals expected Gilmore to plead guilty. In fact, Comstock, in a talk at the First Baptist Church of Elmira, revealed that he had urged Gilmore to admit his guilt and hope for leniency from the courts. He said to Gilmore, "You have got yourself into serious trouble, plead guilty and throw yourself upon the mercy

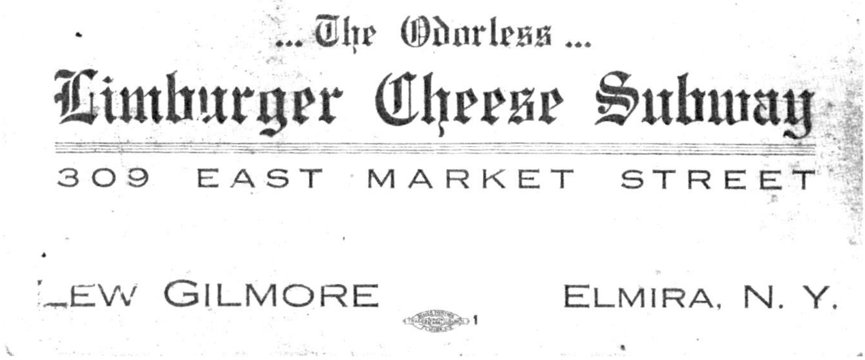

... The Odorless ...

Limburger Cheese Subway

309 EAST MARKET STREET

LEW GILMORE ELMIRA, N. Y.

Above: Trade card for Lew Gilmore's "Odorless Limburger Cheese Subway," one of his many businesses.

Right: The reverse of the trade card features one of Gilmore's unusual poems, but this one is not obscene.

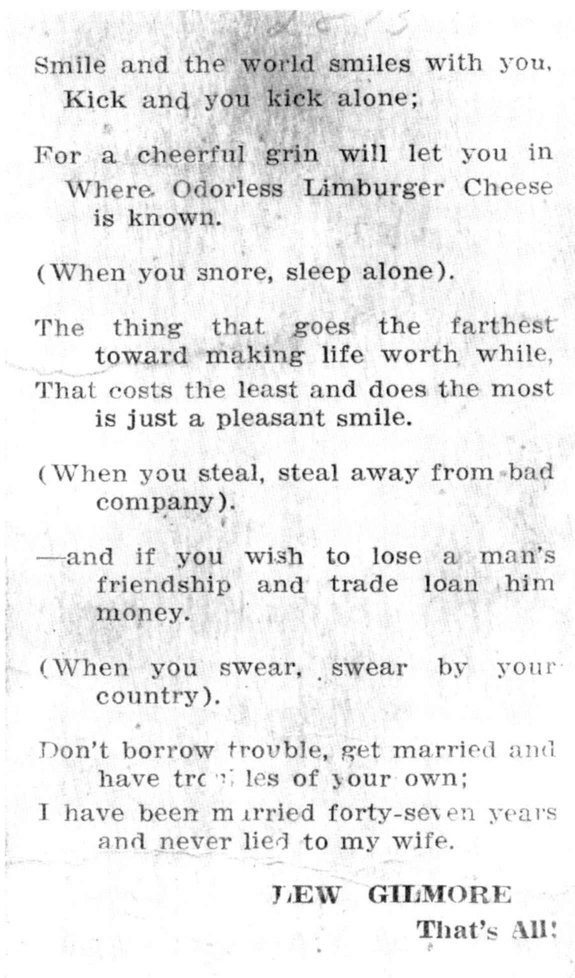

Smile and the world smiles with you,
Kick and you kick alone;

For a cheerful grin will let you in
Where Odorless Limburger Cheese is known.

(When you snore, sleep alone).

The thing that goes the farthest toward making life worth while,
That costs the least and does the most is just a pleasant smile.

(When you steal, steal away from bad company).

—and if you wish to lose a man's friendship and trade loan him money.

(When you swear, swear by your country).

Don't borrow trouble, get married and have troubles of your own;
I have been married forty-seven years and never lied to my wife.

LEW GILMORE
That's All!

of the court and you will find that all the court officers will treat you kindly." Gilmore followed Comstock's advice.[97]

The court fined Gilmore fifty dollars. With that, the federal ordeal was over. Charges were apparently dropped against the Harrison brothers. In March, all of the men were tried in county court, but if there were any punishments, they were mild.

Gilmore's arrest and trial seemed to have little lasting impact on his reputation. By the end of 1894, mentions of Gilmore in the local news were positive. He threw a large Thanksgiving party for friends and formed a group he named the Ancient Order of Blue Men—his favorite color was used for a satirical bit of wordplay on the popular fraternal group the Improved Order of Red Men. Despite his troubles earlier in the year, it was reported that "Lew Gilmore is the soul of geniality."[98]

In January 1895, the *Deruyter Gleaner* claimed that Comstock was charged with attempted blackmail of Gilmore, but this was likely incorrect or a joke. If it was true, nothing seems to have resulted from the charges.[99] The Comstock incident proved to be fodder for jokes for several years, however. An 1898 humorous article made up reasons that prominent Elmirans might enlist in the Spanish-American War. The author speculated that Gilmore would give the following response: "That I might be an Anthony Comstock on the Island and serve corn fed eggs with every 'bier.'"[100]

On March 7, 1898, the Blue Front caught fire. The building was a total loss.[101] Gilmore seemingly took this opportunity to again change trades. He began managing hotels, first the Elmira House and then the Wind Mill Hotel in Pine City, five miles south of Elmira. The Wind Mill became well known for its dinners, due in large part to Gilmore's advertising. In 1907, he moved to nearby Montour Falls to run the Giles House. That endeavor may have been short lived, because in 1908, his name appeared on advertisements selling fireproof and waterproof paint.

In 1910, he established a café at 309 East Market Street in Elmira. As with the Blue Front and the Wind Mill, the café allowed him to personally interact with customers, which was his strength. A review of his new business read, "'Lew' has a way of making his patrons at home and his wit and good humor make him friends by the hundreds."[102] In 1914, he was forced to relocate his establishment to Carroll Street when the building's landlord refused to continue to rent to a business that served alcohol. Gilmore remained a recognizable social figure until his death in 1925. He was buried in Woodlawn Cemetery.

PART III

STRANGE ANIMAL TALES

Nonhuman animals generally do not get as much attention in the historical record as people do, but they played significant roles in our local history. From farms to city streets, animals have been workers, companions, pests and more. What follows are four instances in which local animals captured public attention for notable, often tragic, events.

8

THE LAST LABRADOR DUCK?

The Labrador duck (*Camptorhynchus labradorius*) was rare and little understood even before the species went extinct in the nineteenth century. A coastal bird, it was found between the eastern coast of Canada and the Chesapeake Bay. The last confirmed Labrador duck was killed on Long Island in 1875. However, the report of a Labrador duck shot in Elmira in 1878 has cast an enduring, mysterious shadow on the story of the species. While many believe that Elmira marks the location of the extinction of the duck, the story becomes more suspect upon closer examination.

The commonly told local myth goes as follows: On December 12, 1878, the Chemung River was flooding its banks. Water was spilling into the Southside neighborhood known as the Buttonwoods. A young boy went out hunting for food for his family and shot a strange duck. Somehow, word of the kill reached W.H. Gregg, a local pharmacist, who rushed to inspect the specimen. However, all that remained were the head and neck. The last Labrador duck unceremoniously became someone's dinner.

This tragic, yet quaint, tale has been told since 1891. Some people have challenged the story's veracity, citing the fact that Elmira is far inland from the duck's known coastal habitat. The prevailing theory to explain the duck's possible appearance in Elmira is that it blew in with the storm that caused the flooding. This is possible, but it would have been an unusual occurrence. However, since no one has challenged any of the other facts of the story, this chapter intends to do so.

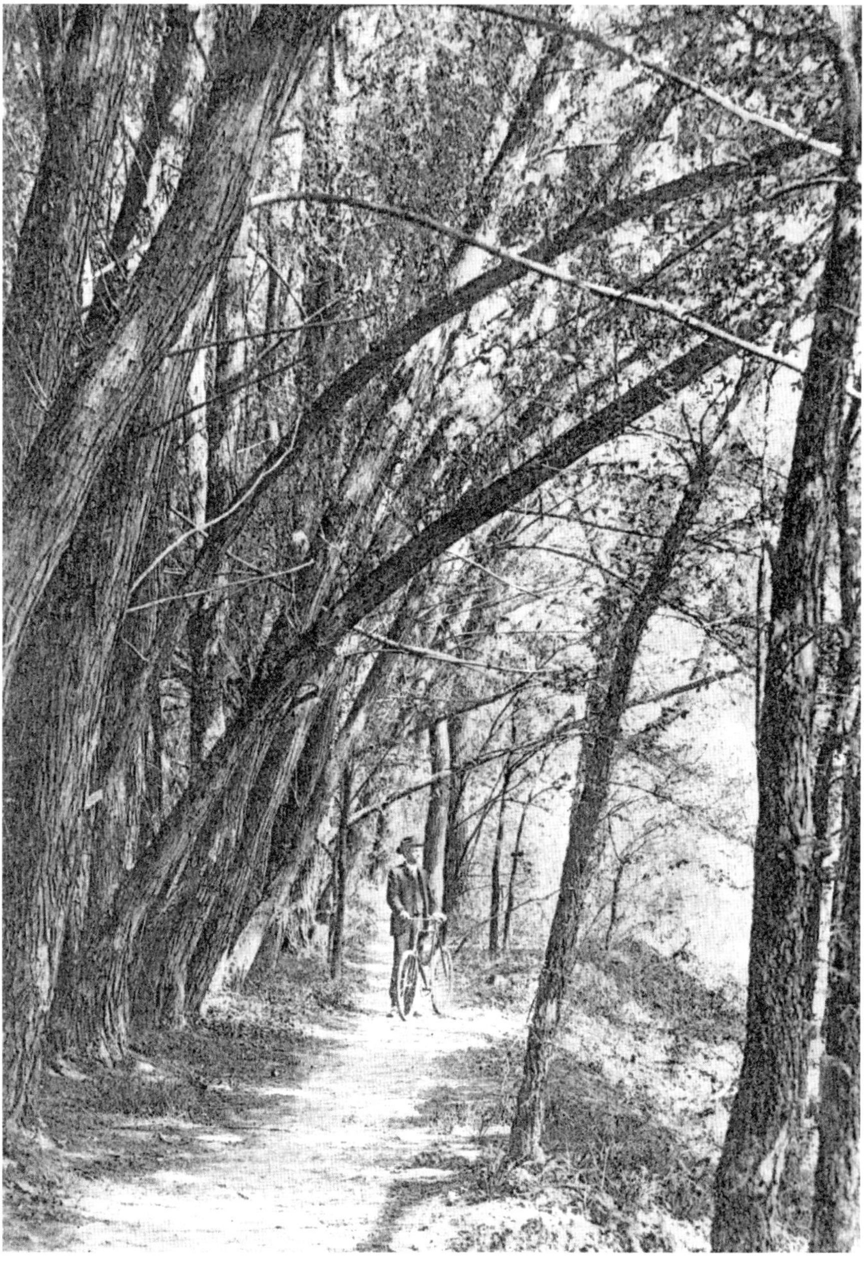

Postcard showing the Buttonwoods, a neighborhood where the Labrador duck may have been killed. It was named for its many buttonwood, or sycamore, trees.

The first record of the Elmira Labrador duck incident was in a brief blurb written by Gregg and published in the *American Naturalist* in February 1879. It read: "The first specimen of C. labradorius (pied duck) known to occur in this locality was taken December 12, 1878. It is interesting, as it adds one more species to the list of birds of Chemung County, N.Y., and assists in clearing up the geographical distribution of the species. C. Labradorius is rare everywhere, and its occurrence so far south in the interior gives special interest to the subject."[103] The report provided no additional information.

Gregg's story was ignored in the Elmira press, but it did earn a brief mention in the *Watkins Express*, a newspaper from nearby Watkins Glen. That report added a pertinent detail missing from all other accounts: the name of the shooter. That February 13, 1879 report stated: "Mr. Waldo Albro, of Elmira, recently shot a wild duck of a species unknown to this part of the world, which he presented to Dr. Gregg, of that city, who had thus made note of it in the *American Naturalist* for February."[104]

If it is true, the *Watkins Express* story radically alters the myth of the local duck shooting. Waldo Albro was most likely William W. Albro or his son Walter H. Albro, neither of whom were "lads" in 1878. William was a Southside cigar manufacturer who lived on Maple Avenue, not far from the area of the alleged shooting. His son Walter, who was around thirty-six years old in 1878, was a bookkeeper. This account also has Albro presenting the specimen to Gregg, a far less romanticized version of the story than Gregg realizing that the duck had been consumed by a family ignorant of the ornithological importance of their meal.

In fact, William Albro was far from ignorant about birds. He was a champion poultry keeper who won awards for his silver pheasants, Aylesbury ducks, turkeys and black Hamburg chickens at various state and local poultry association shows from the 1870s to the 1890s. While his knowledge of domestic birds does not necessarily mean that he could identify an atypical wild species, he may have recognized that the bird was not a native species to the area and not eaten it.

The role of Dr. William H. Gregg, the recorder of the duck's presence in Elmira, is another mystery that bears further examination. His writings and statements form the basis for all of the subsequent retellings of the extinction story. What were his credentials? Gregg was a pharmacist, doctor and all-around scientific investigator who graduated from the College of Physicians and Surgeons of New York in 1857. He served as a surgeon in the Civil War and then worked as a druggist. Gregg's early pharmacy work was not

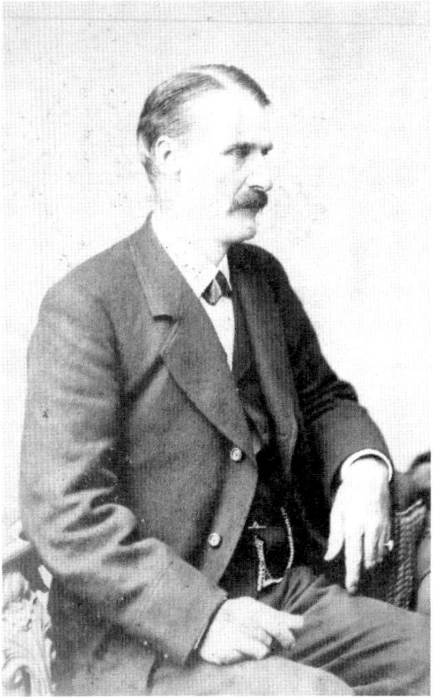

Portrait of Dr. William H. Gregg.

without incident. In December 1866, the "most terrific and devastating fire ever known in the history of Elmira" began in the basement of Gregg's pharmacy at 12 Lake Street. The blaze eventually engulfed twenty-four neighboring stores and businesses, resulting in a loss of $500,000.[105]

Beginning in the 1860s, Gregg also gained a reputation as an authority and authenticator of questionable local scientific claims. In 1869, he examined the water from a so-called medicinal spring on the site of a new resort, declaring it to have "remarkable curative properties."[106] He did not find every specious claim that came across his desk true, however. Sent a sample from the Taughannock Giant, a large stone man found near Trumansburg, New York, in July 1879, he said it was a fraud and that "the whole thing has the appearance of a clever trick."[107]

At the same time that Gregg was supporting or debunking others' claims, he was working on his own dubious business venture. By 1865, Gregg began peddling his patent-medicine concoction "Constitution Life Syrup," which he claimed could cure a long list of ailments, including "Diabetis [*sic*], Gravel, Diseases of the Kidneys, Dyspepsia, Painful Menstruation and Female Irregularities."[108] By 1878, he added the patent-medicine "Electro Silicon" to his offerings.

Gregg's snake-oil business decisions went beyond basic fraud. In March 1878, Gregg found himself deeply embroiled in the Bank of Chemung scandal. The bank, the second oldest in the city at that time, closed its doors without warning one day and never reopened. The bank reportedly had possession of over $400,000 of customers' money at the time of its closing. Bank owner Harry Beadle fled Elmira under the cover of darkness. Upon further investigation, authorities discovered that Beadle had been overdrawing accounts for his personal gain and colluding with friends and local businesses so they could do the same. One of the main accomplices in the scheme was W.H. Gregg & Company. The firm's account was overdrawn

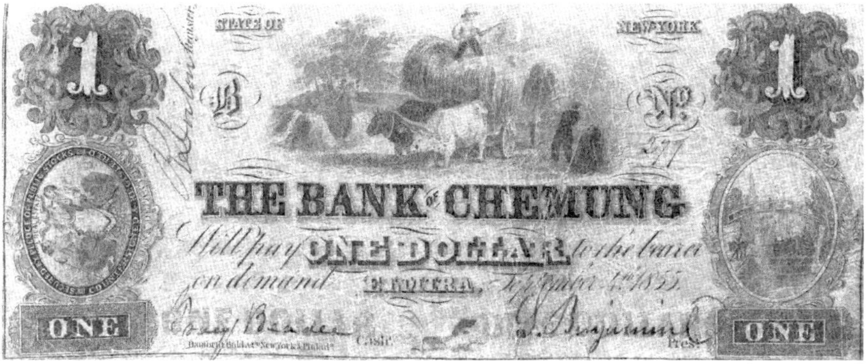

A one-dollar bill from the Bank of Chemung.

by $51,790. The *New York Times* reported that W.H. Gregg & Company was "a firm of local druggists, and the fact has been made public by a judicial investigation, which is now in progress, that Beadle was the 'company' of the firm." The pair used most of the money to advertise Gregg's patent medicines in newspapers around the country.[109]

By April, judicial action was proceeding, and Gregg was arrested for refusing to testify. A judge later overturned the arrest. [110] The ensuing legal battle was a mess of suits and countersuits. Creditors were offered a settlement of thirty-three and one-third cents on the dollar on their investment, and many apparently took the deal.[111] Gregg seemingly faced no significant legal repercussions for his involvement, but by September 1878, he had sold his pharmacy business.[112] Perhaps he needed the money to pay his legal debts and any required repayments.

The Bank of Chemung chaos happened several months before the reported Labrador duck incident. By that December, the fallout from the scandal would have softened, but Gregg would not have been the most trustworthy man in Elmira. His history of fraud does not necessarily mean that he also lied about the duck, but the possibility must be entertained.

Other than the brief notice printed in the *American Naturalist*, no one paid much attention to Gregg's claim in the years following his supposed sighting. There seem to be no references to anyone wanting to see the proof or anyone further investigating the claim. In 1880, Gregg released his *Revised Catalogue of the Birds of Chemung County, New York*, an updated listing of birds he first published ten years earlier. Among the book's 218 listed birds, entry 201 is the Labrador duck. Gregg wrote: "The occurrence of this species in this locality must be entirely accidental. It was formerly common on our coast as far south as Long Island, but is now on the verge of extinction. This specimen was taken after the terrible gale of Dec. 11, 1878."[113] Again, no mention was made of the story of the boy, the duck being eaten or the status of the specimen.

In July 1880, the Nuttall Ornithological Club reviewed Gregg's catalogue. Its take on his work was critical, and the review claimed that many of the new birds listed were done so "upon doubtful authority." But it did commend the corrections of "many errors" Gregg had made in his first edition. One of the most egregious of those earlier errors was the false identification of a new type of bird, *Collyrio chemungensis*, or the rufous rumped shrike.[114] The bird turned out to be a juvenile great northern shrike. The incident does beg the question, if Gregg misidentified a bird once, could he have also misidentified the supposed Labrador duck?

In 1891, William Dutcher, the authority on the Labrador duck and future president of the National Audubon Society, published a catalogue of the existing specimens in North America. The Elmira duck is listed under his "Specimens Recorded and Since Lost" section. When Dutcher contacted Gregg about the specimen, Gregg relayed that it had been lost when he moved to New York City. He said he "entrusted the packing of his specimens to another person" and that the head was accidently "thrown away with some moth infested birds as of no interest or value."[115] Gregg in fact had moved from Elmira to New York City in 1882, where he worked as a drug appraiser in the New York Custom House.[116] The next year, he controversially was denied a position as an examiner of drugs after failing his civil-service examination. With the specimen's disappearance, however, no one of any authority on the matter was ever able to authenticate the find. Dutcher's report may also be the first time that Gregg told, or at least had printed, the version of the story involving the "lad" shooting and eating the bird. After this was printed, it became the prevailing narrative of the Elmira duck.

Ultimately, the story of the extinction of the Labrador duck remains a mystery. Could the last duck have been killed in Elmira? Maybe. The sum of the evidence available casts doubt on parts of the story, but unless definitive evidence is found to prove either version, we will never know. Regardless, Elmirans have embraced the myth. Sculptor Todd McGrain installed a large sculpture of the Labrador duck in Elmira's Brand Park as part of his Lost Bird Project. This project aims to memorialize extinct bird species in the locations where they were last seen.

9

THE ELDRIDGE PARK BEAR PIT

Elmira's beautiful Eldridge Park, founded in 1870, included manicured gardens, classical sculptures and a bandstand. However, the park also held a darker attraction: a bear pit. The first pit opened in the summer of 1891, and the park housed bears for forty-three years. The legacy of the pit is one of violence.

The pit, constructed at a cost of $2,031.41, was thirty feet across and approximately eleven feet deep and lined with brick, cement and stone.[117] It was modeled on Roman gladiatorial amphitheaters, and viewers had to climb stone stairs to reach the top, where they could look down into the circular pit. Dens were built into the mound for the bears, which could climb the cedar trees planted in the center. Two black bears were the first inhabitants.

The bear pit was immediately controversial. Some people felt that the pit was too expensive and was draining the city's finances.[118] Safety was also a concern. In August 1891, an enthusiastic young tourist from Pennsylvania nearly fell into the pit. As the *Elmira Daily Gazette and Free Press* reported, "he was rescued with but the loss of his hat, and while the *Ursus Americani* made tatters of his head-geer [*sic*], he was led away, meek eyed and shame faced, but prayerfully thankful that the bears had nothing more animate than a twenty-five cent hat to exercise their jaws upon."[119] Park commissioner T. McCarthy Fennell was vocally opposed to the pit. Citing its danger, poor construction and design flaws that made it difficult to care for the bears, he advocated the pit be replaced with iron cages. Fennell argued that the pit

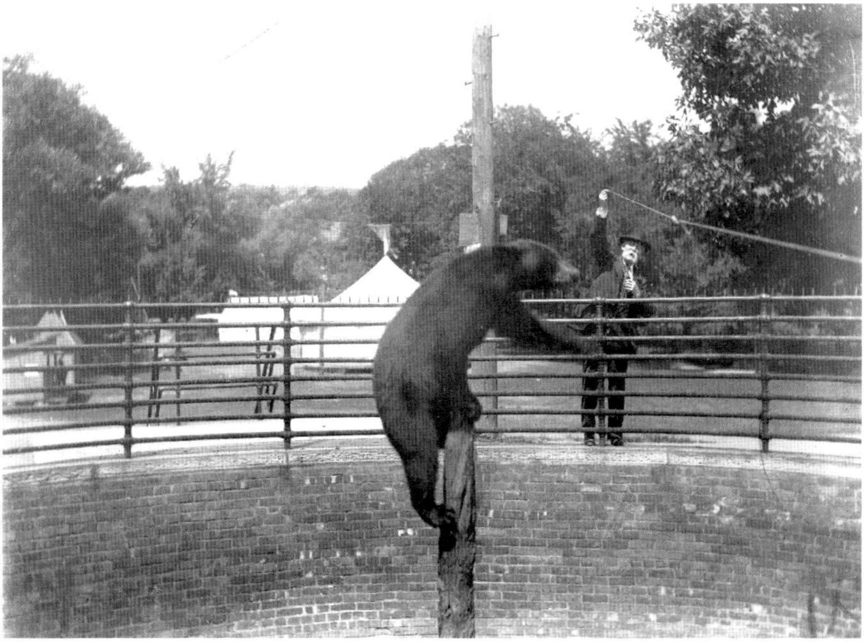

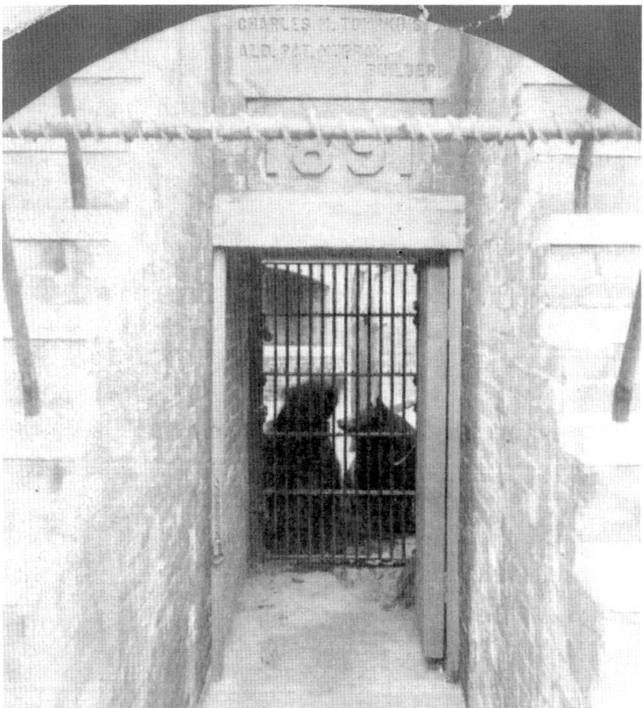

Above: The bears in the pit had limited options for engagement with anything resembling their natural habitat.

Left: Bars and railings kept visitors out of the bear pit.

could be converted into storage or "a musee or chamber of horrors."[120] His opinion was unpopular, and the pit remained.

Fennell was correct in his observation that the pit was not an ideal habitat for the bears. Visitors delighted in tossing peanuts to the bears, but during some Fourth of July celebrations, more deviant revelers threw firecrackers into the pit. On July 4, 1892, a bear tolerated an assault by fifty young men "until a large cannon cracker exploded uncomfortably close to his head, when he seemed to lose all interest in the Glorious Fourth and retreated to his own private quarters."[121] On the holiday in 1909, boys were found "torturing" bears with firecrackers, sticks and stones. The disgusted report in the *Elmira Star-Gazette* read, "Frightening the animals with dynamite crackers is about as mean a thing as could be done."[122]

However bad the threat from visitors was, the greatest hazards to the bears came from within the pit. The bears were not able to follow their natural hibernation patterns in the enclosure. Observers noted this fact but were not alarmed by it. Instead, many took this as a sign that the bears in the pit were displaying more civilized behavior than those in the wild. A 1903 report noted: "His Bruinical Lordship persists in sitting up and noticing things all winter. This is accounted for by the fact that the bear pit is deep and fairly warm all winter and the need for hibernation is done away with."[123] This myth persisted until the 1930s and the closing of the pit. A 1930 article noted how "civilized" bear Tessie was, since she did not need to do the "primitive" act of hibernating. Tessie reportedly only slept at night because "people are constantly calling."[124]

The most serious danger to the bears came from fights. While it was unlikely that there were organized bear fights, the bears maimed and killed one another frequently, a byproduct of their constant and close confinement. One of the first major fights occurred in August 1895, when a Rocky Mountain black bear killed a small cinnamon bear. When the keepers arrived on the gruesome scene, they had to fight the larger bears off the cinnamon bear with iron poles. The cinnamon bear died later that day from his or her injuries.[125] In October 1903, a large female bear killed a young male bear who had been added to the pit the month before. The battle left him "a mass of torn and bleeding flesh upon the cement floor of the pit."[126] The same female bear had killed or disabled at least two bears prior to that incident.[127]

Spring was a particularly deadly time of year for the bears, with some people commenting on the occurrences of the "annual spring fight." An April 1906 fight claimed the life of a female bear and left "Mr. Bruin" alone

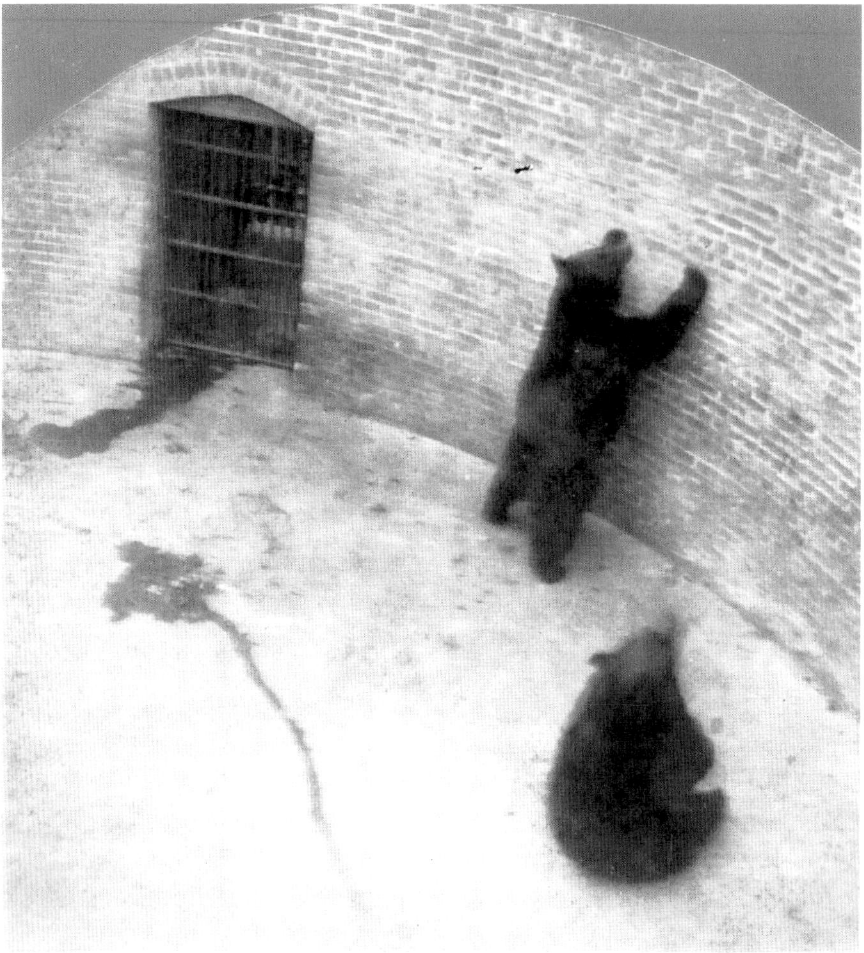

View of the bear pit from above, showing how it was devoid of materials from the bears' natural habitat.

"with no wife to growl at or mate to fight. The fatal fight was a catch-as-catch-can affair and went to the finish. If it was a family jar, it probably resulted from a bear hug."[128] In March 1911, three ursine siblings fought; one was left "mangled and nearly devoured by the other two." The bears had been purchased from Maine as cubs, and the park commissioners hoped that the remaining bears could get along without further carnage so as to not necessitate placing a new cub order.[129]

By 1905, people began to complain about the failing condition of the pit. One disgusted visitor wrote a letter to the *Elmira Telegram*:

> *The condition of the bear pit is a disgrace to the city. The iron railing around the pit is corroded badly and with a big crowd hanging on is apt to give way precipitating many into the pit. A few damage suits will no doubt result. The iron railings and stone steps leading from the bear pit are also badly broken. I also observed an odor from the pit.*[130]

Foul odors, broken stairs and corroded railings were just part of the problem. The decaying conditions of the pit allowed one bear to escape. In January 1909, a bear managed to get out and walk the streets undetected until it encountered Thomas Parkinson, who was walking home from his job as a Lackawanna Railroad switchman, at a crossing around 7:00 p.m. Parkinson swiftly turned around, and some reports claimed he ran all the way home to Elmira Heights. The incident was actually the second time the bear had gotten loose in three weeks. On its previous adventure, it ate three pigs on Davis Street.[131]

In 1912, the city finally made the necessary changes to the pit and redesigned it for increased safety. They leveled the mound, making a flatter surface from which viewers could look at the bears at eye level instead of from above.[132] M.R. Ellis, president of the Humane Societies, was encouraged by the changes. Although he maintained that "any sort of confinement

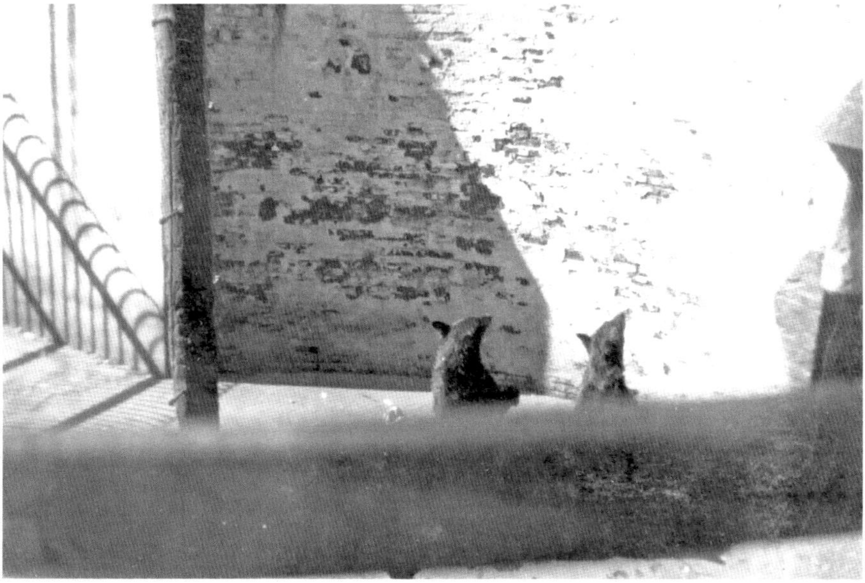

The bear pit in 1923, eleven years before it closed.

is unnatural to the wild animal," he praised the park, stating that it had turned the pit "from an egregious mistake into a commendable addition, in its efforts to instruct and amuse the people....There was no possible excuse for the old pit." He urged that this new change be used as a way to instruct children on the importance of kindness to animals.[133]

In the 1910s, the park continued to purchase bears from Maine, where they were raised for sale. In May 1914, the purchase and arrival of three four-week-old black bear cubs caused great local excitement. They were first displayed in the window of a local store, where they were fed warm milk. When they were a little older, they were brought to the pit.[134]

Bears were added to the pit until September 20, 1934, when Tessie, the last remaining bear, died. She was approximately twenty years old. During the Great Depression, maintaining the pit was no longer financially feasible, and no new bears were added. In 1937, parks superintendent Fred A. Wright proposed using the vacant pit to house monkeys, but that idea seemingly gained no traction. In April 1940, the pit was demolished as part of a Work Projects Administration project to build Eldridge Park Road.[135]

10

BOB THE SEA LION

In mid-June 1903, Bob the sea lion escaped from his habitat at Trout Park in Cortland, New York. It was not the first time he had broken out; he got loose about a month earlier but was recaptured shortly after in the town of Marathon. His second escape was more successful, and for over a month, the wily sea lion swam through various rivers in New York and Pennsylvania, eluding all attempts at capture. However, his fortune changed when he reached Elmira, where his escape ended in tragedy.

When Bob first fled from Cortland, he entered the Tioughnioga River and swam south. He was spotted in nearby Messengerville, but according to a report, "the lion was crafty."[136] Bob continued floating down the Tioughnioga and then entered the Chenango River where the rivers converge at Chenango Forks. Near Chenango Forks, people made a failed attempt to capture Bob with wire nets stretched across the Tioughnioga. The attempt was thwarted, as it had recently rained, and the water level rose enough for Bob to easily swim over the net.[137]

Once in the Chenango River, Bob continued his way south to the city of Binghamton, where he was reportedly sighted on June 22. Bob's distraught trainer, Nelson Pike, traveled to Binghamton from Cortland to attempt to capture the escapee. By this time, Bob's owner, Jack Boone of Syracuse, offered a reward for the safe trapping of the sea lion, whom he valued at $1,000. Pike fretted that Bob would grow weak from exertion and a lack of saltwater fish. He implored people to use the utmost care when attempting to catch Bob, saying he posed no danger to humans. Pike believed that if only he could get near Bob, the sea lion would respond to his voice and come to him.[138]

Journalists covered every Bob sighting and, by July, began joking about the ongoing situation. The *Rome Daily Sentinel* opined: "Any one who possesses a sea lion should be careful to keep the animal well enclosed, not because it might bite somebody, but because when once it gets free and finds a good stream of water it is a very difficult thing to capture....Sea lions are handsome pets, but they have their disadvantages."[139] The *Genoa Tribune* reported that Bob was "still sailing on" because "Cortland has too small a pond for him."[140]

In Binghamton, Bob entered the Susquehanna River and followed it into Pennsylvania. In mid-July, he was reported in Sayre, Towanda, Wyalusing, Laceyville, Meshoppen, Wilkes-Barre and even as far south as Sunbury. Some of these reports may have been false, however, because some misinformation about Bob's adventure was printed and later discredited.

During the Pennsylvania leg of his swim, Bob became the center of a strange rumor. For some reason, portions of the Chemung and Susquehanna Rivers turned red. Farmers supposedly collected the dark red water to use instead of paint for their barns. A prevailing theory for the alarming color change was that Bob was the cause; it was reported that "sea lions when too persistently pursued exude a reddish matter that is, when put to paper use, stronger than any glue."[141] Others more rationally noted that, even if it was true, one sea lion could not excrete enough to stain entire rivers.

At some point in Pennsylvania, Bob reversed course and headed into the Chemung River. When he swam through the town of Chemung, people were so excited that they abandoned their farms and places of work to watch him. On July 23, he was seen in Elmira. A reported three thousand people crowded the riverbanks, and five hundred men attempted to capture him.[142]

The fun ended on July 25. That day, John "Stub" Appleton, his son John Jr. and Charles Bucholtz got in a boat and managed to corner Bob in shallow water near a dam. As they tried to wrestle Bob into the boat, John Jr. clubbed Bob in the head until he died. The men claimed that the 150-pound sea lion attacked them and they killed him out of self-defense.[143]

People were outraged about the senseless killing. His former trainer, Hugh Sharpe, was interviewed by local press. "I could not feel worse if some one pointed a gun at my heart and knew that they would pull the trigger.... People will think that foolish, but that is the way I feel about it. It is the same affection I have for 'Bob' that a man has for his faithful dog who has been with him from a puppy."[144]

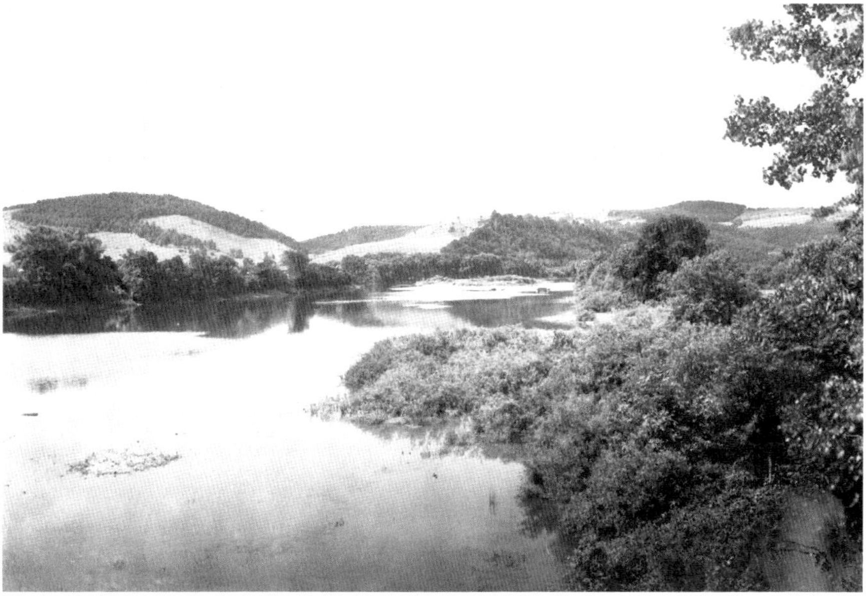

The Chemung River as seen from the Walnut Street bridge, early twentieth century.

Citizens of Cortland were most enraged, decrying "the stupid, brutal conduct" that "deprived one of God's creatures, of almost human intelligence, of its innocent life." The *Elmira Telegram* described the melancholy scene at Trout Park in Cortland, where children gathered to pay their condolences to Duchess, Bob's mate. Reportedly, "one pretty tot of a girl was sure that she saw tears fill the eyes of the Duchess…and the little one extended her pocket handkerchief that the Duchess might becomingly wipe away her widow's tears."[145]

Bob's dead body was put on ice and sent via train to his owner in Syracuse. Once there, Boone refused to pay the fifty-dollar shipping charge; Bob had to be returned to Elmira. Back in Elmira, the body was reportedly stuffed and put on display in a local store window.[146] Boone planned to file a lawsuit against the killers and to have the body returned to him. It is unclear if this ever happened. He also noted that he planned to order more sea lions from California but would also buy some alligators.[147]

Thus, with an act of violence and an undignified battle over his corpse, the journey of Bob the sea lion concluded. During his month of freedom, Bob brought great joy to people along miles and miles of river. But, at the same time, his story illustrates how the history of human and animal interaction is frequently punctuated with brutality and heartbreak.

11

THE PIGGERY PROBLEM

For much of its history, Elmira has had a serious problem with garbage. Until the early twentieth century, there were no municipal garbage disposal services. Rag and bone pickers collected saleable scraps, and herds of pigs roved the streets eating food scraps that residents tossed from their windows. In 1905, locals protested the city council's proposal to build an $18,000 incinerator that would have provided municipal garbage disposal for the city. Instead, the Bennett Incinerating Company, a private firm, handled garbage collection, but its service was expensive and excluded many residents. As trash piled up in the city, the local government struggled to find a comprehensive solution. Unsanitary conditions were blamed for disease outbreaks, and in 1916, local newspaper columnists opined that trash could lead to cases of infantile paralysis, or polio.[148] By 1917, some Elmirans began proposing a novel solution to the problem: a piggery.

The *Elmira Star-Gazette* ran a story in August 1917 about a piggery in Hull, Massachusetts, suggesting it as a possible cure for Elmira's garbage crisis. In the piggery system, a city's food and digestible trash was fed to pigs. Once fattened, the pigs were sold at market. The city could theoretically make a profit on its trash.[149] The conversation about a local piggery picked up in 1918. Champions of the piggery saw it as a patriotic wartime endeavor. The state's department of health urged the city to consider a piggery, as the swine could be used to produce much-needed animal fats and oils for the war effort. Noting that the system might not make the most financial sense, supporters argued that "even if the piggery shows a small loss each

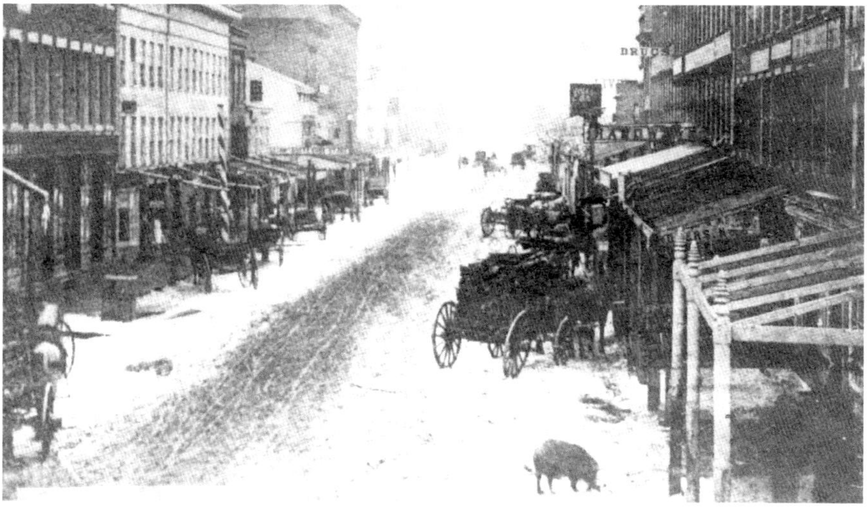

A pig on Elmira's streets, circa 1860s. Before organized trash collection, pigs roamed the city, eating trash that people dumped onto the streets.

year, the people of Elmira will be more than willing to pay the very slight additional tax knowing that the city has done its part in supplying a war need."[150] Others argued that the city should not be hasty with the piggery decision, that it had not been investigated thoroughly to see if it would even work for a city the size of Elmira. Still, the voters denied another proposal for an incinerator, and the common council vowed to further investigate the piggery option.[151]

A year later, the city was ready to move ahead with the piggery. The main argument in favor of this system was that it would allow the city to offer free garbage collection to all residents, including those in poor neighborhoods who had never had trash services. The system was imperfect, however. The city would still need to build or contract with an incinerator to burn the garbage that the pigs could not eat. The pigs would also need to be slaughtered at another site. There were fears that having a large concentration of pigs might lead to outbreaks of hog cholera, which would "add heaps of festering swine-flesh to the garbage heaps."[152] The project ultimately needed to be approved by the city's board of health.[153]

By September 1919, the proposed piggery was a source of increasing conflict in local meetings and in the press. Much of the criticism of the plan centered on the fact that the city planned to work with private companies and farmers instead of creating a true municipal system. Local farmer Leon Drake submitted a bid to have the city's garbage brought to his farm on South Creek Road, on the south side of the Chemung River. Drake, however, insisted that the city pay for the trash collection and delivery and that he be awarded a twenty-five-year contract for his services. Opponents estimated that this would cost the city tens of thousands of dollars each year.

Elmiran Myer H. Friendly led the charge against private ownership of the piggery with an open letter in the *Elmira Star-Gazette*. Friendly threatened to start a taxpayers' action against the city should the proposal advance. In other cities, piggeries were run without additional expense to citizens because they were city-owned. The crux of Friendly's argument was that the city should not have to pay private companies for the garbage collection services. Friendly and his supporters argued that "if some arrangement could be made to insure that a considerable part at least of the cost of collection would be paid by those deriving the benefit of it through the piggery, then opposition to the plan doubtless would disappear."[154] A cartoon published in the September 14, 1919 issue of the *Elmira Telegram* furthered the argument that the proposal was unacceptable.[155]

In late September, the board of health said it would reject Drake's proposal in its current form. At the time of his submission, he had not yet officially formed a company, despite the fact that he was already trying to sell stock.[156] Drake wrote a letter to the mayor withdrawing his proposal.[157] The board of health claimed that it was abandoning the piggery effort unless another proposal emerged.[158] Still, the piggery issue was far from dead. On October 10, 1919, the *Star-Gazette* published an antagonizing letter by Drake asking Friendly if he'd take $5,000 worth of stock for the piggery on the Drake farm.[159] Mayoral candidate George Peck included a platform opposing a private piggery in his political advertisements.[160]

The Murphy Process Company of Buffalo stepped in to resurrect the piggery proposal. The company chose to contract with Drake to use his farm as its location, and it hired Elmiran Daniel Livens to do the collecting. The proposal was accepted by the city, but it was controversial. The project remained in the development stage until 1922. When the piggery was about to begin operation, neighbors on Elmira's south side lodged complaints that the runoff would drain directly into their properties, poisoning their wells. R.B. Walsh, a resident of Fulton Street, claimed that the side effects of the planned piggery would unfairly target impoverished neighborhoods, stating, "too many people are trying hard to down the poor man today."[161]

By this point, the piggery had fully infiltrated local culture. On March 24, 1922, the *Elmira Star-Gazette* published the poem "It Is Only Natural," which read:

When a city adopts
The piggery plan
Probably there is
A scrap among the
Pigs when the garbage
Arrives from the
Aristocratic section
Of the City[162]

Upon learning that the city was requiring residents to purchase garbage cans to comply with the piggery collection, department stores ran huge sales on bins and supplies.[163] The piggery reportedly created a boom in store sales.[164]

Garbage collection for the Murphy Process Company's piggery began on June 1, 1922. The system cost the city $8,000 per year, or approximately $1 per family, not counting the cost shouldered by citizens for the proper garbage cans. Residents had to comply with a strict two-can system: one for foodstuffs and one for inedible material. The board of health would conduct patrols and arrest people who improperly disposed of trash.

The project was doomed from the start. When collection began, the company still had not built any housing for the pigs.[165] And none was ever built. The company merely bought herds of pigs and set them loose on a large lot where garbage was given to them from tank wagons, to the chagrin of neighbors.[166] Less than a year later, on February 9, 1923, the Murphy Process Company abandoned its contract, claiming it was financially unable to continue. The company's demise affected the entire region. Not only had it established the Elmira piggery, but it also had contracts in the nearby towns of Waverly, Bradford, Bath and Hamburg. Investors were said to have lost as much as $100,000.

With the Murphy Process Company out of the piggery business, the city continued the venture with collector Dan Livens, who wanted to establish his own piggery on Mount Zoar Street on the south side. As of March 23, 1923, he had forty pigs and planned to have three hundred soon. When he took over the piggery, Livens said he would charge the city $27,000 a year, but he offered to do it for $18,000 on the condition that the city sign a five-year contract and provide a place for garbage disposal. Livens and the city struggled to agree on the terms.

Again, residents of the south side protested and tried to convince the city to prohibit the establishment of a piggery within three miles of the city limits.[167] Dr. Ernest G. Treat, the Town of Southport's health officer, declared

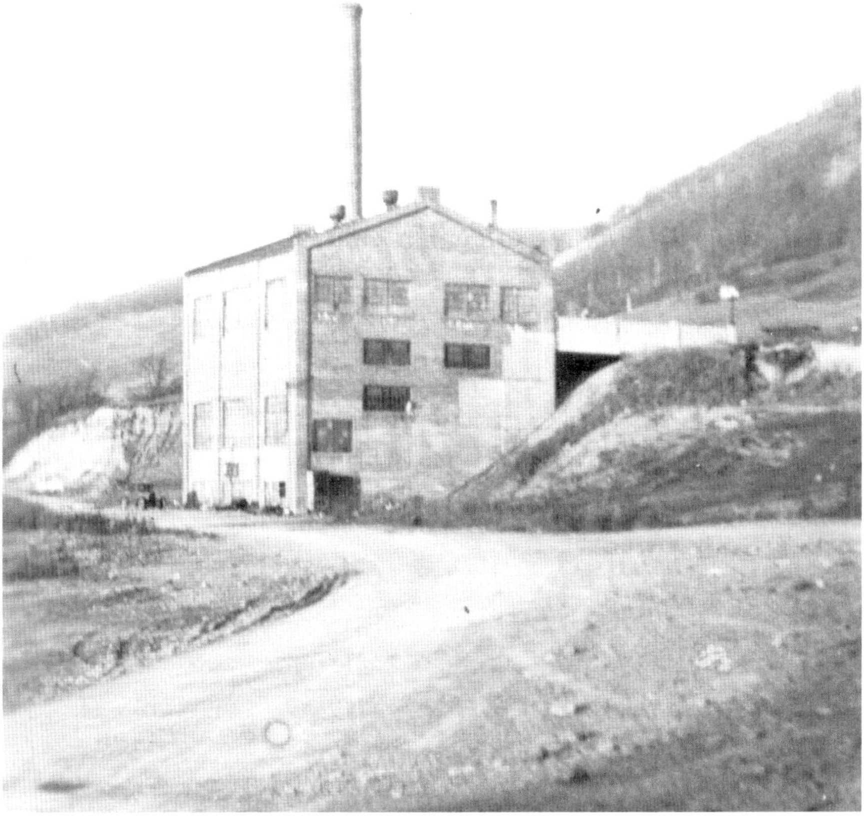

The trash incinerator built after the failure of the piggery.

Livens's piggery a nuisance, saying that the runoff and odors were dangerous to residents' health. The board of health did not sustain his opinion, and the mayor failed to act, since the piggery was technically outside the city limits.[168]

By June, city officials abandoned the piggery and the concept of free garbage disposal. The city again turned to privatized garbage collection, this time from the Bennett Incinerating Company (then the Banfield-Jennings Company). Although many officials still believed a public option was possible, the piggery ordeal had soured Elmirans on the idea.[169] After exploring a few other options, the city purchased farmland beyond the city limits and began burying the trash there. As with the piggery, this system caused significant problems for neighbors. It was abandoned when the city finally built an incinerator in the 1930s.

PART IV

THE SUPERNATURAL

Elmira was on the eastern fringe of the burned-over district, the area of western New York famous for religious revival in the early nineteenth century. Amateur preachers in the sparsely populated frontier created new religions, including Mormonism and Millerism. Among the new religious movements was spiritualism, which began with the Fox sisters of Hydesville, New York. Beginning in the 1840s, they sparked a frenzy and gained followers and notoriety with their claims that they could communicate with the dead through mysterious rapping sounds and séances. Despite the vocal protests of skeptics, by the end of the nineteenth century, spiritualism was popular in Elmira. Believers could attend local spiritualist churches or gatherings and consult clairvoyants. The spiritualism movement was predicated on people's belief that the dead could speak to the living. This set the stage for ghost stories that fascinated and terrified Elmirans throughout the nineteenth and twentieth centuries.

12

SPIRITUALISM, CLAIRVOYANTS AND MAGNETIC HEALERS

In 1876, C.L. Jennings, who had briefly worked as a medium in Elmira, wrote a full confession of his dishonest spiritual dealings in an effort to discredit spiritualism. It was printed in the *Rochester Union* on September 18. Jennings said, "From my past experience of spiritualism and mediums, I am willing to swear before God and man that every medium I came into contact with were frauds of the deepest dye." After coming to Elmira from Virginia, he had an encounter with an alleged medium and decided to debunk such otherworldly communication. He used the guise of being a medium himself to perfect the tricks that produced the rapping and ringing sounds that passed for proof of ghostly presence. He held private séances and earned the endorsement of local mediums. He hoped that the fact that he was able to fool these "experts" would prove enough evidence to "restore to reason and consciousness the poor benighted, demented, idiotic humanity that have been so long dupes to this preposterous belief, and of so called mediums."[170]

Jennings's confession did little to sway the opinions of true spiritual believers. He cited a local clairvoyant physician, Mrs. R.H. Wilcox, by name as one of the supposed mediums he had fooled, but she maintained a successful practice until her death in 1883.[171] She saw patients from around the region, diagnosed them simply by looking at or briefly touching them and prescribed remedies that made liberal use of gin.

Wilcox had devoted clients and her business survived Jennings's attack, but she was not immune to the criticism and pranks of other local skeptics. The *Geneva Courier* reported that some of Wilcox's letters and the

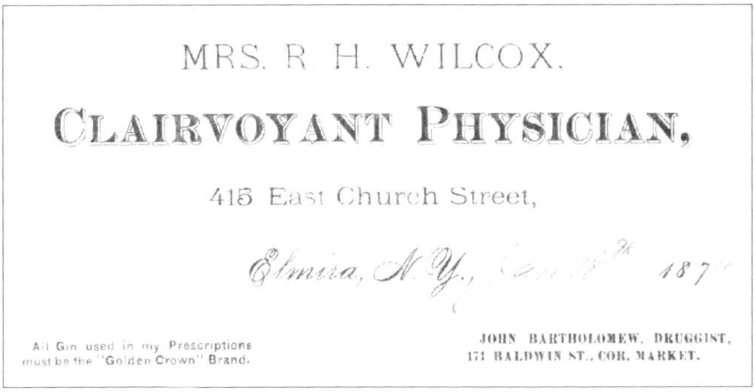
MRS. R. H. WILCOX.

CLAIRVOYANT PHYSICIAN,

415 East Church Street,

Elmira, N.Y., 187

All Gin used in my Prescriptions must be the "Golden Crown" Brand.

JOHN BARTHOLOMEW, DRUGGIST, 171 BALDWIN ST., COR. MARKET.

Letterhead used by clairvoyant physician Mrs. R.H. Wilcox.

money in them sent by her "misguided patients" were stolen from the post office. Having fun at Wilcox's expense, the paper noted, "she knew what was the matter with a person by looking at a lock of his hair and by squeezing a fellow's hand he became transparent as clear water to her eyes—but stolen money and filched letters were not her line."[172]

Vienna Allen, referred to more frequently as Mrs. J.E. Allen, was another of Elmira's renowned clairvoyants. Born in Tompkins County on December 31, 1841, she displayed clairvoyant talent as a child. Although both her mother and paternal grandfather were mediums, her great-aunt once tried to "whip the devil out of her" for claiming that she "saw the pretty folks." Vienna married John E. Allen on March 10, 1862, and worked professionally as a medium. She was a renowned business medium and counseled local businessmen on the soundness of their investments.[173] She maintained regular office hours, held special message meetings and spoke to crowds. She died at her family home at 705 Pattinson Street on March 5, 1920.[174]

Mary Stroman was Vienna Allen's contemporary and primary competitor. Like Allen, she worked as a general and business medium and had a practice in the city. She had a reputation for accurate predictions and was even consulted by the parents of Harry Smith, a murdered man from Hornby, New York. When the press learned of the unusual meeting, Stroman said:

> *I do not know anything I told Mr. and Mrs. Smith, when they called upon me yesterday afternoon....I told them not to say anything about me that would get me into trouble....I only tell what I see and hear. I am here to do good and not bad. I do not give names unless I hear them. Has there been anything bad in the papers about me?*[175]

She worked as a medium for about thirty years before her death at age eighty in 1924.[176]

Stroman was also one of the founders of the First Spiritual Unity Society of Elmira, which was active by the 1890s. There were earlier spiritualist groups, like the Chemung County Spiritual Society, which formed as early as 1871. But the First Spiritual Unity Society was the largest and best organized.[177] The *Corning Journal* even noted the growth of nontraditional churches, writing, "among the church notices in the Elmira newspapers, is one of the First Spiritual Society, one of the Spiritual Light Society, and one of the Christian Science Society."[178] The spiritualist church combined ideas of traditional Christianity with its mission of providing "unbelieving and doubting minds evidence of a continual and an immortal existence, and of a continued intercourse and relationship between the living and the so-called dead."[179] Meetings consisted of lectures, medium readings and demonstrations.

In 1902, the society hired Mary C. Von Kanzler of Indianapolis, Indiana, to be its reverend. She was well known in the field and had twenty-five years of experience.[180] Von Kanzler and her church were controversial for many people, especially the leadership of other churches. Reverend William Van Allen of Grace Episcopal Church gave a lecture titled "Evil Spirits and Their Present Day Manifestations," which attacked spiritualism. He did not deny that people could communicate with spirits. But, he claimed:

> *when a medium was not a fraud or a mind reader, he was assisted by an evil spirit from the other world, and that instead of spirits of the dead really returning to give messages to the living, the Devil himself deceived the medium and other people in order to turn their faith from the true teachings of the Catholic Church.*

Von Kanzler addressed Van Allen's speech in front of a crowd of several hundred people. She was uncompromising in her criticism, stating, "Father Van Allen must be an evil man or he could not have spoken so much about evil." She said, "We believe in Christ and in the Bible. The Lord was a clairvoyant….This priest says that all the spirits about us are evil….Do you believe that when your dear ones come back to give messages to you that they are evil spirits?"[181] Ultimately, the criticisms seemed to have had little effect on the group, which remained active until at least the 1920s.

In addition to clairvoyants and mediums, Elmira also had people working as magnetic healers. Although magnetic healers did not claim to communicate with the dead, their alleged supernatural powers functioned like those of clairvoyants. Similar to Mrs. R.H. Wilcox's claims to be able to diagnose a person just by looking at them, magnetic physicians said they could diagnose and heal patients by touching them and transferring magnetic energy. Frank E. Lyon was a well-known and well-regarded magnetic healer in Elmira in the early 1890s. His many testimonials from satisfied customers reported that "a simple, light stroke of the doctor's hand over the body will convince a person that he is possessed of a great power as a magnetic healer."[182] Other reports claimed that Dr. Lyon was not "associated with various 'healers' and blustering physicians who go about the country under the guise of religious miracle workers, spiritual mediums and unscrupulous physicians," because he was born with the gift of magnetism that he could use to heal most ailments.[183] Among his success stories was his cure of eleven-year-old Floyd Stratton of Addison, New York, who had been unable to use his left hand for three years. After Floyd received his first treatment, which consisted of Dr. Lyon moving his hands over the child's fingers, "the doctor dropped a tooth brush on the floor and requested him to pick it up. The boy took the brush in his hand, which had been helpless so long, and it was with difficulty that it could be removed from his grasp."[184] Three treatments later, the boy was supposedly completely cured.

Lyon's base of operations was in Elmira, but he did frequent short residencies and consultations in surrounding towns and even opened an office in Addison in 1893. In fact, it was his actions during one of those traveling visits that got him into serious legal trouble and seemingly ruined his career. In April 1892, Lyon was at the Luther House in Naples, New York, peddling his cure for "rheumatism, paralysis, nervous prostration, dyspepsia, liver and kidney diseases, inebriation, loss of manhood, female diseases, fits, etc., by magnetism."[185] The next year, he was charged with bastardy for fathering a child with a young Naples patient, Cora Desmond. (It is possible that he fathered the child during the April 1892 visit, but it could have happened during another residency.) Desmond's age at that time is unknown, but one report stated that she was eleven.[186] On November 25, 1893, a constable went to arrest Lyon, who was working in Watkins Glen. Lyon denied the charges, but the people of Naples judged him guilty at trial and in the court of popular opinion. He was sentenced to pay to support the child.[187] After the trial, advertisements for Lyon's magnetic practice disappeared from the local newspapers.

Dr. Isaac C. Dow came to magnetic healing as a second career. Originally the master car builder at the Fall Brook machinery shop in Corning, New York, he quit his job around 1879 after discovering his ability to cure disease with his innate magnetism.[188] He moved to Elmira and opened a practice, earning "the confidence and esteem of his patients and of those who knew him."[189] His practice apparently flourished, enabling him to purchase a large new hotel near Elmira in 1882.[190] He continued his practice until his death at age seventy-five on May 19, 1899, at his home at 714 West Water Street.

Other magnetic healers opened up shop in Elmira or visited for brief demonstrations of their abilities. "The Boy Phenomenon," a young magnetic healer of national fame, visited Elmira in 1898 and set up a temporary office at 113 West Second Street. Hundreds of Elmirans visited, and the young man supposedly cured locals of such ailments as incurable bladder troubles, deafness, paralysis, asthma and heart disease.[191] In 1875, Dr. Hale, a self-styled "Wonderful Magnetic Healer," worked at 218 Baldwin Street and claimed to cure chronic diseases without medicine.[192]

Not all magnetic doctors were well received, however. A Dr. Delmeta "stepped out" after perhaps not being able to deliver his "astonishing cures" in 1880.[193] More than twenty-five years later, questionable magnetic healers earned the ire of Mayor Zebulon Brockway, who reported that he saw an increase in requests to establish magnetic practices in the city. Brockway informed the solicitors that there were no laws prohibiting such businesses, but he told them it was against the "moral law" and he could not support fleecing "simple minded people" of their money.[194]

The services of magnetic healers and clairvoyants fell out of fashion by the early twentieth century. While some continued to practice and spiritual churches continued to conduct meetings, the practitioners no longer garnered the same attention from either supporters or detractors.

13

GHOST STORIES

In 1905, concerned residents of Elmira's east side were convinced that there was a haunted house in their neighborhood. People reported hearing strange noises coming from the vacant house at 750 East Church Street during the night. Paranoia spread as neighbors told stories about the ghosts residing in the building. Most people avoided the house out of fear, but a few mustered the courage to inspect the house. Their investigation yielded an unexpected result: a group of young boys had broken into the building and were taking great delight in toying with the superstitious neighbors. The police were called, and the "ghosts" were dispersed.[195] While the eastside haunted house proved to be the result of childish mischief, many Elmirans still believed that spirits existed.

On January 19, 1880, the *Elmira Daily Advertiser* skeptically told of a supposed haunting of the Washington Avenue bridge. The newspaper conceded that the visibility of the bridge made it a better location for "ghostly habitation" than did "vacant houses or antiquated mansions that stand back from the highway."[196] People observed a female spirit with long hair and a flowing dress dancing across the bridge, illuminated by the nearby fires burning at the Elmira Rolling Mill. The *Daily Advertiser* posed several alternate theories for the sightings, ranging from plausible to ridiculous. The Elmira Female College was located near the bridge, and the newspaper reported that "it is possible that what has been seen was some unhappy young lady of the College unfortunately given to somnambulism, and who nightly goes to the Bridge in her retirement

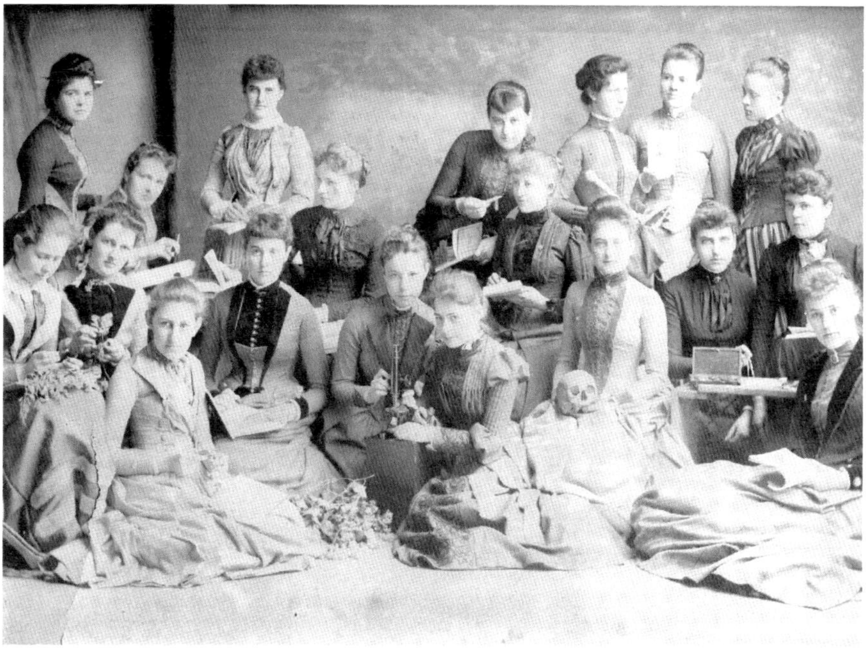

Elmira College students, 1880s.

apparel, to see the cars go by, and innocently and incidentally to bewilder and frighten unsuspecting wayfarers."

A second theory facetiously suggested that the students had secretly invented a flying machine in their room and took turns sneaking out at night to test their invention. Therefore, the ghost was simply precocious college girls riding their experimental airship and spooking innocent bystanders. The newspaper also suggested that the whole matter could be resolved if the next witness investigated the haunting rather than ran away screaming.

Another of Elmira's reported specters favored another piece of local transportation infrastructure: the trolleys. In 1888, the *Elmira Telegram* published a report on a mysterious veiled woman who rode the Clinton Street trolley line nightly toward Governor David Hill's home. The woman was reported to appear on the trolley without the vehicle ever stopping. She brought with her "an icy vault-like gust of air that seemed to congeal the marrow in the bones of the crowd."[197] Clad in black from head to toe, she spoke the name of her stop with a "monotone, hoarse, sepulchral, and absolutely unwomanish—almost inhuman—voice." The coin with which she paid her fare was always gone in the morning. A curious group of men

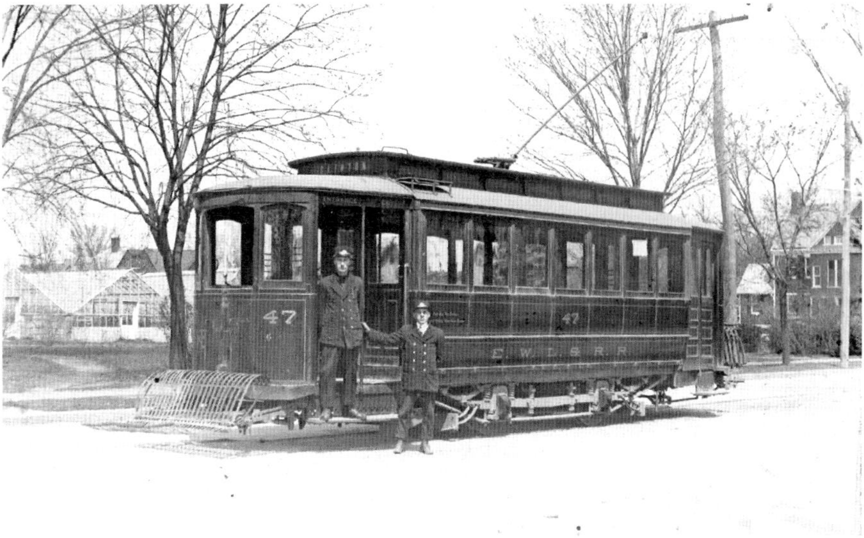

The Clinton Street trolley.

followed her after she departed the trolley one night and reported that she floated down the street, only to disappear suddenly.

The former Wilcox Hotel at the corner of Hudson and James Streets on Elmira's south side was a worn and dilapidated building by 1897, when the *Elmira Daily Gazette and Free Press* reported on the supernatural activity rumored to take place there. People heard odd noises and saw unusual shadows in the windows. Forty years earlier, the hotel had been a hotbed of gambling, rowdiness and crime. Two deaths added to the former hotel's supernatural mystique. A man had been killed by falling timber, and a player in a contentious game of cards had died of a broken neck under suspicious circumstances. The hotel closed and the building was converted to apartments, but many tenants were forced out by unexplained sounds and apparitions. Neighbors reported seeing a ghostly figure fall from an upper window every midnight. When the *Daily Gazette* investigated, the owners, Mr. and Mrs. Klein, disputed the claims, with Mrs. Klein saying she thought the whole matter was the result of pranks and the expected sounds of the tin roof. Still, just the week before, one of Mrs. Klein's friends claimed to see a ghost on the property, causing her to run screaming for safety.[198]

In 1908, residents near the Second Street Cemetery reported a "spook" wandering between the headstones. The mysterious female ghost seemingly had no destination or purpose, but just appeared when it was dark enough.

Some neighbors remained skeptical, but others were convinced that the old cemetery was haunted.[199]

Some ghost stories played on the racial stereotype that African Americans were more superstitious. In 1910, Lorenzo Lee, a black porter in a West Water Street barbershop, ran screaming from the basement of the building, where he had been checking the furnace. He claimed that a ghost had grabbed him. Lee pointed to the coal-stained handprints on the back of his white coat as evidence. The newspaper used the incident to comment on his race and presented his refusal to return to the basement in dialect.[200]

Elmirans have largely forgotten these ghost stories, but other tales persist today. Some students claim that Elmira College's oldest buildings are home to supernatural residents. The former site of the Elmira Confederate prison camp is also a popular location for paranormal investigators.

PART V

ELMIRA'S FAMOUS CHARACTERS

There have been many famous Elmirans, even if their names are no longer remembered today. Some of these people earned fame for their intelligence, skill, humor or even their strangeness. Many were part of Elmira's rich theatrical scene. Grand theaters lined the city's streets in the late nineteenth and early twentieth centuries, and Eldridge Park and Rorick's Glen attracted traveling shows from around the world. Some performers traveled widely, showcasing their talents and seizing opportunities not available to the average citizen. However, fame could have a dark side. Discrimination, exploitation and tragedy could often be found beneath the glitz and glamour.

14

THE HOTCHKISS WOMEN

Each member of the family of Thomas W. and Jean Hotchkiss, including their children Thomas and Bessie, was talented and well known in his or her own regard. But the women stand out in particular. Thomas W. Hotchkiss and Jean Jewell were married on December 3, 1863. Their daughter, Jeannie Elizabeth Hotchkiss, better known as Bessie, was born on July 25, 1865, and son Thomas was born on January 29, 1867. The family lived a privileged life, financed largely by Thomas Sr.'s success in the lumber trade. He was involved in the early years of the LaFrance brothers' company. He financed the Jeannie Jewell engine, named for his wife, that helped save the company. Even before their marriage, both Thomas and Jean came from wealthy families. This prosperity helped Jean and Bessie achieve success and notoriety not reached by many women in the nineteenth century.

Jean Jewell Hotchkiss was born near Utica, New York, on May 24, 1837. Her family's wealth afforded her an education at the Buffalo Seminary and lessons from renowned tutors in drama, elocution, voice and Shakespeare. At eighteen, she began giving public readings. Reading, or elocution, was a popular type of performance in the nineteenth century. The reader would take the stage alone and work without any of the usual trappings of a play or other performance, like props, costumes or sets. Jean was particularly well known for her readings of Henry Wadsworth Longfellow's *Hiawatha* and Lord Tennyson's "Enoch Arden." Her early performances also featured work by William Shakespeare, Edgar Allan Poe, Charles Dickens and Richard Brinsley Sheridan.

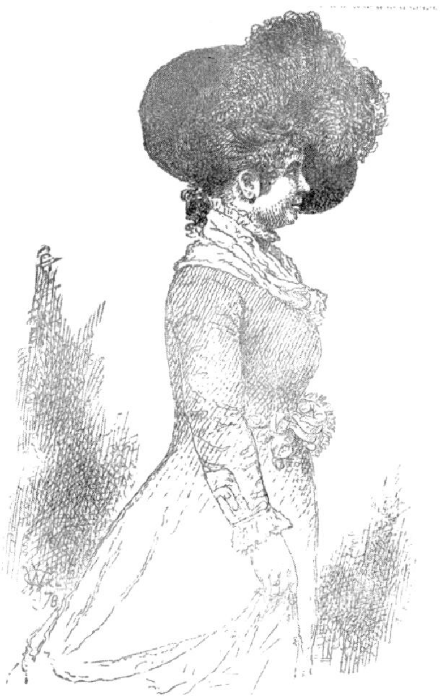

Portrait of Jean Jewell Hotchkiss, as drawn from a painting by George Waters.

The young Jean soon made her reputation in the crowded field of elocution. An 1859 letter from a member of her audience in Fort Plain, New York, noted:

> *Miss Jewell, instead of standing or sitting at a desk, appears upon the stage without book or prompter, and by proper and becoming action, gives increased effect to the author's words. That she is perfect we do not claim, but that any one with not more than two years' reading, and probably not over 40 or 50 readings, can excel her, we do not believe.*[201]

Readings were a feat of endurance, and her shows could last for two hours.

Jean was gaining considerable regional fame, but she left the stage to care for her family when she married in 1863. Her hiatus was short lived, however. By the mid-1870s, she was touring again. She issued a publicity brochure in 1874 to book venues for a tour starting that December. The brochure featured pages of testimonials from newspapers and prominent figures attesting to the quality of her work. An excerpt from the *Pittsburgh Evening Chronicle* read, "She is a lady of rare personal attractions, dresses with elegance and taste, and is, in social circles, a lady of culture and refinement. Her rendering of Enoch Arden would have delighted the poet LAUREATE." The *Albany Argus* claimed, "Her beaming countenance, lit up with genius, her resplendent eyes and commanding figure, remind one forcibly of the World's Nightingale, the charming Jenny Lind." Praise from the *Cortland Gazette* read, "She is so versatile in her delineations, that one almost forgets the 'Jewell,' and believes that a whole troupe of artistes are appearing in a role of characters."[202]

The tour successfully restarted her career, and she performed in larger venues and cities. On February 17, 1875, she performed at Steinway Hall in New York City. After a brief respite at Gleason's Water Cure Sanitarium in Elmira for an undisclosed illness in November 1875, she continued

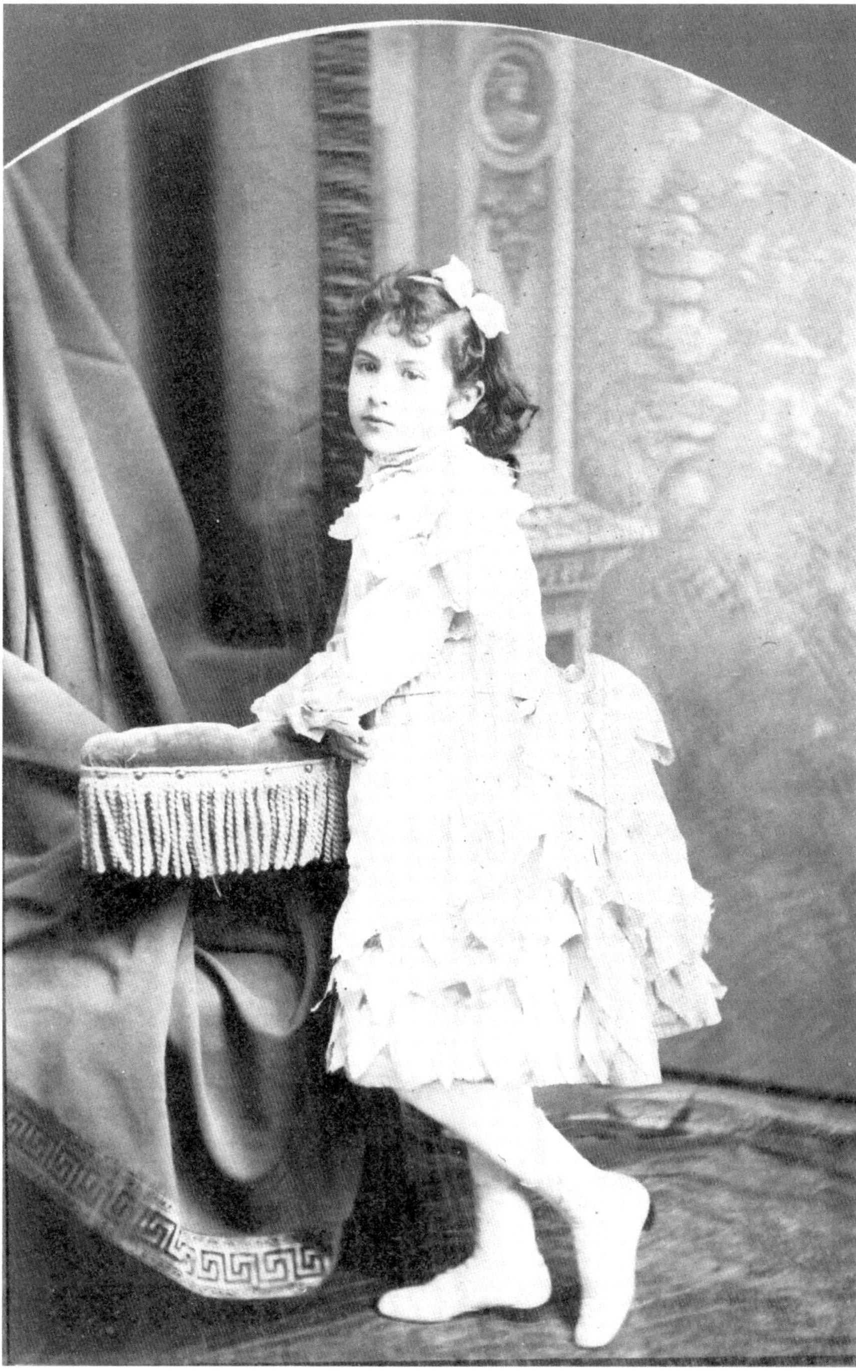

Bessie Hotchkiss as a child.

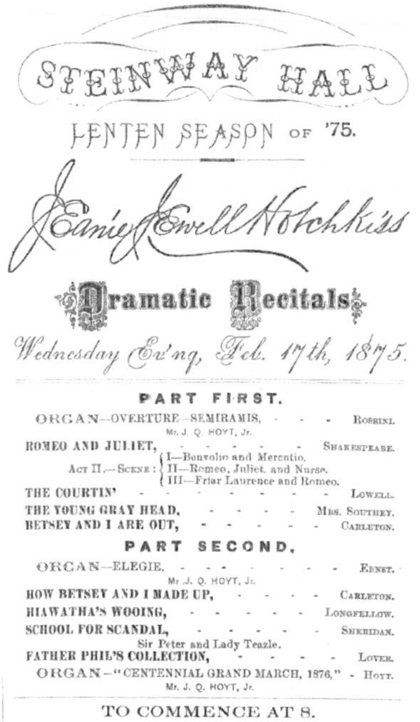

STEINWAY HALL

LENTEN SEASON OF '75.

Jeanie Jewell Hotchkiss

Dramatic Recitals

Wednesday Ev'ng, Feb. 17th, 1875.

PART FIRST.

ORGAN—OVERTURE—SEMIRAMIS, - - - ROSSINI.
Mr. J. Q. HOYT, Jr.

ROMEO AND JULIET, - - - - - - SHAKESPEARE.
Act II.—Scene: I—Benvolio and Mercutio. II—Romeo, Juliet, and Nurse. III—Friar Laurence and Romeo.

THE COURTIN' - - - - - - - - - LOWELL.

THE YOUNG GRAY HEAD, - - - - MRS. SOUTHEY.

BETSEY AND I ARE OUT, - - - - - - CARLETON.

PART SECOND.

ORGAN—ELEGIE, - - - - - - - - - ERNST.
Mr J. Q. HOYT, Jr.

HOW BETSEY AND I MADE UP, - - - - CARLETON.

HIAWATHA'S WOOING, - - - - - - LONGFELLOW.

SCHOOL FOR SCANDAL, - - - - - - SHERIDAN.
Sir Peter and Lady Teazle.

FATHER PHIL'S COLLECTION, - - - - LOVER.

ORGAN—"CENTENNIAL GRAND MARCH, 1876," - HOYT.
Mr. J. Q. HOYT, Jr.

TO COMMENCE AT 8.

Program for Jean Jewell Hotchkiss's performance at Steinway Hall on February 17, 1875.

working.[203] Reviews of her shows were typically positive, but in the competitive world of elocution, there were some exceptions. A December 5, 1878 show in Medina, New York, earned the following review: "The Dramatic Recitals by Jeanie Jewell were well attended, but she greatly disappointed her audience. The best part of the entertainment was the music by Brainard & Dodd's orchestra."[204]

By the early 1880s, Jean's career options had grown, and she partnered with actor Frank Mayo. Mayo was well known for his folksy portrayal of Davy Crockett. In 1881 and 1882, she toured with Mayo and starred in Shakespeare plays. Instead of reading, she apparently acted the parts of Lady Macbeth in *Macbeth* and Emelia in *Othello*. The Mayo-Hotchkiss partnership was reportedly fraught with tension, and they stopped working together when they failed to reach any agreements.

While Jean occupied the stage, her daughter, Bessie, also began to make a name for herself. Known for her beauty and charm, Bessie was also ambitious and intelligent. She was privately educated in Elmira in her youth and then attended Elmira College. She received her bachelor's degree in 1887 and her master's degree in 1889.

In 1889, the entire family accompanied Thomas Sr. to Ottawa, Canada, where he was appointed a position as consul. The intelligent, gregarious and beautiful Hotchkiss women were the talk of the Ottawa social scene. Bessie, in particular, took full advantage of both the social and political offerings in the city. She attended sessions of Canadian Parliament and received invitations to important parties and gatherings. In an interview with the *Elmira Telegram*, Bessie spoke highly of her experience in Canada: "The ladies are charming. They are stylish and well-groomed, and the men are always interesting, and dignified. They are so well groomed, and so are the ladies for that matter, and they have an easy dignity that American men, in their hurry and rush of business, cannot find time to cultivate."[205]

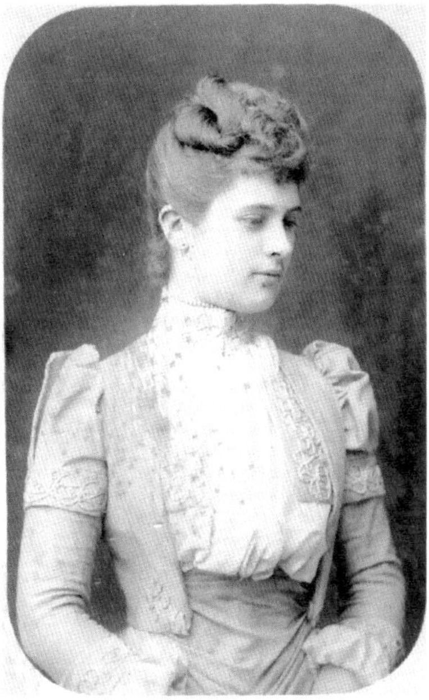

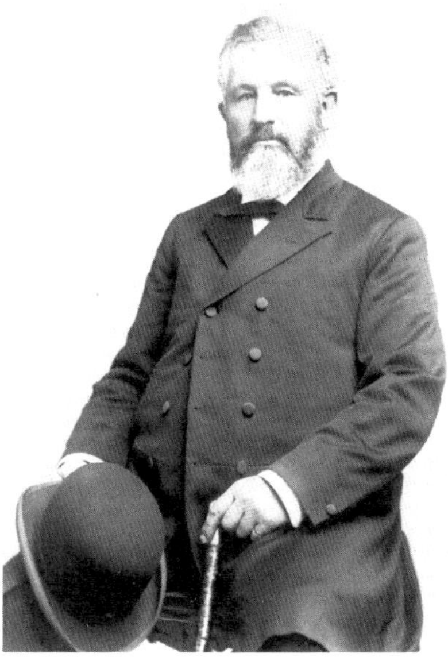

Left: Bessie Hotchkiss as a young woman.

Right: Thomas W. Hotchkiss around the time he was a consul in Ottawa.

While Bessie was making an impression on the international scene, she was also a feature of domestic political gossip. By 1889, rumors swirled that Bessie was engaged to Elmiran David Hill. Hill, twenty-two years older than Bessie, was governor of New York (January 6, 1885–December 31, 1891) and would later serve as a U.S. senator (January 7, 1892–March 3, 1897). The Hotchkiss family and Hill were old friends, and Hill had known Bessie since she was a child.[206] The rumors peaked in 1889, but they persisted for years after. The story of the pair's alleged romance filled newspapers across the country. In 1894, one newspaper joked, "If Senator Hill is ever going to marry it is the opinion of his friends that he should do what he can in the matter of confirming this pleasant rumor."[207]

Bessie and Hill both denied the rumors. Hill even gave angry interviews on the subject after the matter was continuously asked by reporters. A reporter joked that Bessie "is a very charming young woman who will make a splendid wife for some fellow one of these days, but it seems to be up-Hill work that the press is having in engaging her to the Governor."[208] In her personal scrapbook, Bessie clipped and saved articles from around the country about her supposed relationship with Hill. She also kept

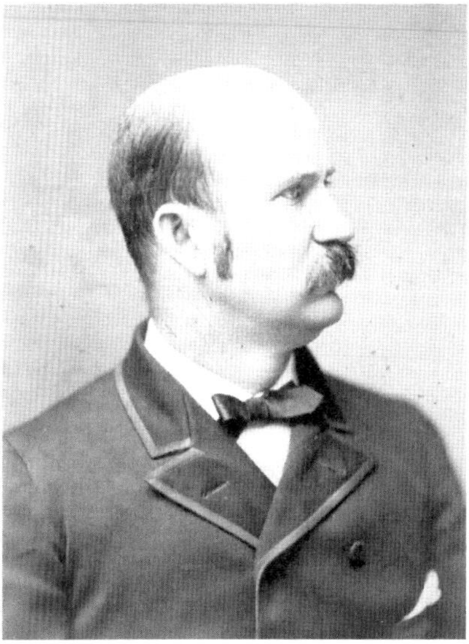

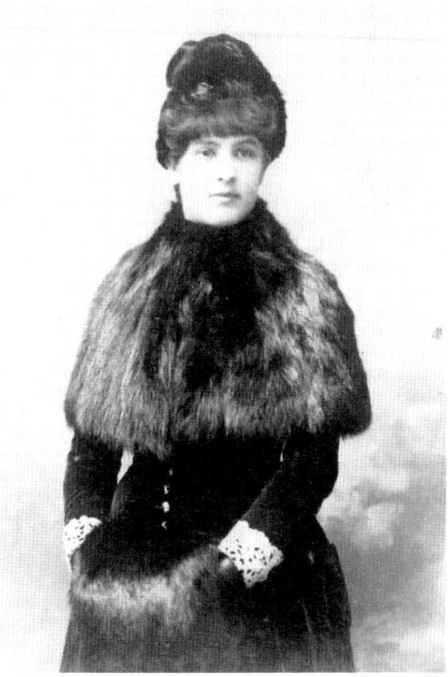

Above: Portrait of David Hill.

Right: Portrait of Bessie Hotchkiss.

other articles about Hill, indicating interest in his career and personal life. On one page of her scrapbook, next to articles filled with engagement rumors, Bessie wrote, "Some little talk awhile of me and thee. There was—and then no more of thee and me." Although unattributed in the scrapbook, that excerpt is from the English translation of *The Rubáiyát of Omar Khayyám*. It is unclear if the juxtaposition of those lines and the gossip columns about her love life hinted at the truth of the relationship. Neither Bessie nor Hill ever married.[209]

In 1894, Bessie earned her PhD from Elmira College, deservedly refocusing the attention of the news from her personal life to her professional accomplishments. She was the first woman to earn a PhD at Elmira College, and she was reportedly the youngest woman to achieve that degree at all. Bessie's degree was in philosophy, but she also took courses in history, ethics, Latin, French, German, rhetoric and literature.

The *Elmira Telegram* wrote: "So unusual is it that a young woman is both an advanced student and yet so completely escapes the characteristics of the blue-stocking in the perfect rounding of her character that Miss Hotchkiss is a notable example of the student and society favorite in one."[210]

Before and after receiving her PhD, Bessie wrote columns for the *Elmira Telegram* and the *Elmira Daily Gazette and Free Press*, as well as for Elmira

College's *Sybil*. She served largely as a social correspondent, covering, for example, the April 1895 New York City wedding of Eleanore Mayo, daughter of her mother's former acting partner, Frank Mayo.[211]

She also wrote about politics and philosophy, particularly in her New York City letter series for the *Elmira Telegram*. One of her articles in the 1895 Christmas edition of the *Elmira Daily Gazette and Free Press* perhaps gives some personal insight into her perspective of being a trailblazing woman. Writing of "The New Woman," she said:

> *She is independent and industrious and womanly. New York abounds in such as these. They fill every possible walk of life....It is due to her self-reliance as much as to the growing weariness of the men that she now frequently stands when all the seats are taken on the elevated road and never once indicates by even a glance that she may have a furtive desire for a seat....She seems to feel however that certain obligations are imposed upon her, and one new woman at least has had the sense to declare that she will never marry until she is able to support a husband.*[212]

Bessie continued to shatter gender expectations when she was appointed editor of the New York City–based *Metaphysical Magazine* in July 1895. The *Binghamton Republican* printed:

> *The appointment is a theory wrecker. One of the most dearly-cherished theories of man is that woman does not succeed in the severer studies; that she has not been eminent in mathematics, philosophy or metaphysics, that she arrives at conclusions by the hop, skip and jump of intuition and not by the exact processes of reason....The question of sex has nothing to do with the case. The appointment of Miss Hotchkiss was due to qualifications, but incidentally it contributes to the demolition of the theory that woman cannot, owing to the construction of her brain, master the severer studies.*[213]

The magazine also published some of her writing, including her articles "Concentricity: The Law of Spiritual Development" and "La Svengali: A Psychological Study."

Bessie's tenure at the magazine was short lived, however. She resigned after her father died of heart failure on December 18, 1895. She continued writing, worked as a practicing metaphysician and was prominent in academic and social circles. In 1896, Bessie was one of five women suggested by the Elmira press to become the next president of Elmira College. The

Elmira Daily Gazette and Free Press opined that it was time for a woman to be in charge of the first college to grant degrees to women equal to those of men. An article stated:

> *A college president should be an excellent executive, a fine teacher, of noble Christian character, possessed of strong sympathy, rare tact, resolute will, absolute self control, the wisdom of the serpent and the harmlessness of the dove. Is not a woman as apt to combine these qualities in one person as a man?...An Elmira woman president of Elmira College! The probabilities and possibilities of such an event are unlimited.*[214]

Ultimately, neither Bessie nor any other woman was seriously considered for the job by college officials.

Bessie extended her metaphysical practice in New York City to include correspondence courses. She created "The Renaissance School of Applied Metaphysics for the Cultivation of Health and Talent," which was a set of twelve lectures. Classes included psychology, aesthetic development and "metaphysics for wee ones," a class for five- to ten-year-olds. In September 1897, she became the editor of *New Light*, a periodical and correspondence course that seems to have been closely related or created from "The Renaissance School." It was based out of the family's home in Northport, Long Island, and her mother, Jean, served as the editor of the magazine's "department of elocution talks and lessons." Jean also maintained her own business, teaching elocution. Her advertisement noted, "She follows the method practiced by the great Murdock. Pupils may also have the advantage of the latest studies in applied psychology."[215] Jean died on November 30, 1918, in New York City.

Until at least 1911, Bessie continued to work as a metaphysician in New York City. Her last known publication was the article "Judicial Aspects of Mental Therapeutics" in the magazine *Mind* in April 1900. The article was about the connections between mind and body in disease. Her life took a tragic turn in the 1910s. In the 1915 state census, she was listed as a patient in the Middletown State Homeopathic Hospital, an institution that treated mental disorders. Census data indicates that she remained there until her death in June 1934.

15

BOB MACK

Although largely forgotten today, Bob Mack was internationally famous during his lifetime in the late nineteenth century. Mack was born enslaved in Kentucky in 1849 or 1850 and, in his late teens, made his way to Elmira at the close of the Civil War. A talented young man, Mack attracted the attention of minstrel show managers, who hired him for their shows. Working with "colored minstrel" troupes, Mack had more opportunity for profit and travel than many black Americans after the war, but he still had to operate in a world where audiences believed that he was inferior. This is the story of a former slave who found his fame recreating a fictionalized, romanticized version of plantation life.

According to an account of Mack's childhood written after his death, he was enslaved at a plantation in Lexington, Kentucky. A sickly child, he was put in charge of caring for the poultry. It was there he honed some of the skills that would make him famous years later. When the Civil War started, the plantation owner's son went to the front and brought Mack with him as a servant. Mack stayed with the Confederate troops for about two years and was noted to entertain the men between raids with his impressions and singing. Eventually, Mack was captured by Union soldiers, and he remained with them until 1865. He then traveled to Cincinnati with $300 he had earned working for the soldiers and providing entertainment and comic relief. In Cincinnati, he met an old woman who helped him find housing. He stayed in the city for a year. When the old woman died, she left him money.

Mack then moved to Elmira, a socially progressive city in the nineteenth century. A long-standing stop on the underground railroad, Elmira was a popular place for black people to relocate before and after the war. John W. Jones, the most well-known escaped slave to make Elmira his home, is remembered for his work on the Underground Railroad helping others escape to freedom and for his remarkable work burying the Confederate dead from the Elmira prison camp. Elmira's abolitionists formed the Park Church and advocated for emancipation. Perhaps Mack had heard of Elmira's reputation and that convinced him to move to the city.

When Mack moved to Elmira, he met John Washington. Washington had escaped slavery in Virginia and came to Elmira in 1846. He later became Elmira's first black police officer, serving between 1876 and 1889. Washington had a reputation for kindness and must have liked the young Mack, because he adopted him and helped him find work as a barber. Mack married Lucinda Gother, another of Washington's adopted children.

Mack earned a reputation as an entertainer in Elmira. He was an expert at mimicry, specializing in bird calls. This talent sometimes got him in trouble, and "the old man whom he always called 'pop' could not break him of these ways." Mack began entertaining people in saloons. He gained acclaim for his comedy. He was spotted by a traveling showman, who got him to join a minstrel troupe.[216]

Black minstrel troupes were a unique offering in the world of blackface minstrelsy. In the early nineteenth century, minstrels were white actors in blackface who performed grotesquely stereotypical portrayals of black people and glorifications of slave life. Minstrel troupes with black performers emerged during the antebellum period, but they became more popular after the war. There were similarities between the white and black minstrel groups' programs, but there were also key differences. Most of the popular black troupes maintained plantation-themed acts, even after those fell out of fashion for white blackface performers. Audiences saw black troupes as more authentic voices telling these stories, even if the material itself was not an accurate representation of plantation life. Some historians argue that minstrel shows gave black actors some agency not afforded to others, because they could have some control over the content of the show and change the narratives of some of the offensive pieces.[217] Still, former slaves like Mack played roles in shows that fundamentally misrepresented slavery in order to please white audiences. Black minstrels could make good salaries, but the pay was still lower than those of most white performers.

Mack first performed with Jack H. Haverly's Colored Minstrels. He toured extensively with that troupe, even traveling to Europe. Mack developed a specialized act that distinguished him from most other performers: he would dress as a large rooster and perform the many lifelike bird calls that he had practiced for years. Audiences loved his "Hen Caucus" and "Barnyard Scenes" acts. Historians have drawn parallels between the portrayals of animals in minstrel shows and racist views of black animality, and audiences may have interpreted Mack's routine in this way.[218]

Despite the multiple interpretations of his act, Mack was capitalizing on a real talent, and audiences and reviewers responded positively. In 1878, Haverly purchased the rights to another black minstrel troupe, Callender's Original Georgia Minstrels, and combined the two into the alliteratively named Callender's Consolidated Colored Minstrels. Mack became a feature of the show.[219] Reviewers in the cities where the troupe performed frequently singled out Mack's performance for praise. One review stated: "Barn-yard Scenes, by Bob Mack, was a novelty to some portions of the audience at least. His imitations of the language of the hen and rooster were admirably executed, and indeed his costume gave him the appearance of being a large rooster."[220] Another said his performance "was one of the most laughable and grotesquely life like bits of imitation ever seen on the stage."[221]

By the early 1880s, Mack added another component to his act: a live chicken. Reportedly, a boy in Davenport, Iowa, told Mack that he had a chicken that would fight him in his rooster costume. The show manager bought the rooster for $2.50, and Mack trained it. The new act featured a costumed Mack engaging in a faux cockfight with the small bantam rooster. The rooster, named Little Dick, proved to be exceptionally popular with audiences. One report of Little Dick's abilities said that he not only knew his act but also would go to the door and retrieve mail from the mail carrier. Mack trained other chickens, as well, with the goal of creating a chicken circus by 1884. The management had so much faith in the inevitable popularity of such an act that they purchased new barnyard scenery and $2,000 worth of lithographs and offered Mack an extra $150, to be paid when the new act premiered. The management had good reason to be confident in Mack's ability; on a previous trip to England, the Prince of Wales was so impressed with Mack's act that he gave him a gold medal with an engraved rooster and diamonds.[222]

Mack's act with the rooster was frequently billed as follows: "Bob Mack and his Accomplished Bantam Rooster, the Only Educated Fowl in Existence."[223] However, despite Mack's skill, some reviewers and audiences

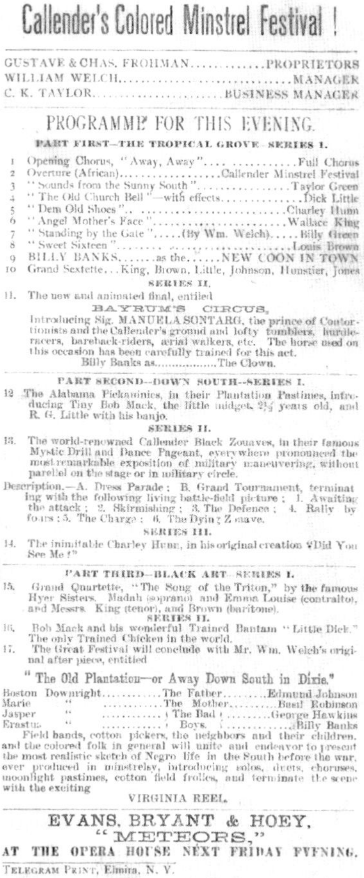

Callender's Colored Minstrel Festival !

GUSTAVE & CHAS. FROHMAN..............PROPRIETORS
WILLIAM WELCH..................................MANAGER
C. K. TAYLOR.........................BUSINESS MANAGER

PROGRAMME FOR THIS EVENING.

PART FIRST—THE TROPICAL GROVE—SERIES I.

1 Opening Chorus, "Away, Away"... ....Full Chorus
2 Overture (African)..................Callender Minstrel Festival
3 "Sounds from the Sunny South"................Taylor Green
4 "The Old Church Bell"—with effects..............Dick Little
5 "Dem Old Shoes".. ....Charley Hunn
6 "Angel Mother's Face"..........................Wallace King
7 "Standing by the Gate".....(By Wm. Welch).....Billy Green
8 "Sweet Sixteen"........ ....Louis Brown
9 BILLY BANKS.......as the......NEW COON IN TOWN
10 Grand Sextette...King, Brown, Little, Johnson, Hunstier, Jones

SERIES II.

11. The new and animated final, entitled

BAYRUM'S CIRCUS,

Introducing Sig. MANUELA SONTARG, the prince of Contortionists and the Callender's ground and lofty tumblers, hurdle-racers, bareback-riders, aerial walkers, etc. The horse used on this occasion has been carefully trained for this act.

Billy Banks as.................The Clown.

PART SECOND—DOWN SOUTH—SERIES I.

12 The Alabama Pickaninnies, in their Plantation Pastimes, introducing Tiny Bob Mack, the little midget, 2½ years old, and R. G. Little with his banjo.

SERIES II.

13. The world-renowned Callender Black Zouaves, in their famous Mystic Drill and Dance Pageant, everywhere pronounced the most remarkable exposition of military maneuvering, without parellel on the stage or in military circle.

Description.—A. Dress Parade; B. Grand Tournament, terminating with the following living battle-field picture; 1. Awaiting the attack; 2. Skirmishing; 3. The Defence; 4. Rally by fours; 5. The Charge; 6. The Dying Zouave.

SERIES III.

14. The inimitable Charley Hunn, in his original creation "Did You See Me?"

PART THIRD—BLACK ART—SERIES I.

15. Grand Quartette, "The Song of the Triton," by the famous Hyer Sisters. Madah (soprano) and Emma Louise (contralto), and Messrs. King (tenor), and Brown (baritone).

SERIES II.

16. Bob Mack and his wonderful Trained Bantam "Little Dick." The only Trained Chicken in the world.
17. The Great Festival will conclude with Mr. Wm. Welch's original after piece, entitled

"The Old Plantation—or Away Down South in Dixie."

Boston Downright............The Father.........Edmund Johnson
Marie " ....The Mother..........Basil Robinson
Jasper " .... The Bad ....George Hawkins
Erastus " .... Boys. ....Billy Banks

Field hands, cotton pickers, the neighbors and their children, and the colored folk in general will unite and endeavor to present the most realistic sketch of Negro life in the South before the war, ever produced in minstrelsy, introducing solos, duets, choruses, moonlight pastimes, cotton field frolics, and terminate the scene with the exciting

VIRGINIA REEL.

EVANS, BRYANT & HOEY,
"METEORS,"
AT THE OPERA HOUSE NEXT FRIDAY EVENING.

TELEGRAM PRINT, Elmira, N. Y.

Handbill for an Elmira performance by Callender's Colored Minstrels in the early 1880s. Both Bob Mack and his son are listed as performers.

drew insulting connections between the pair. One review of the act stated of Little Dick, "In fact, it displays more intelligence in many things than its master." [224]

Mack's "mirth-provoking" chicken performances were situated between more traditional minstrel fare.[225] A handbill for a performance in Elmira in the early 1880s listed performances of African songs, clowning, military demonstrations from the Callender Black Zouaves and the "Alabama Pickaninies." The latter featured "Tiny Bob Mack," Mack's two-year-old son. The event culminated with a piece entitled "The Old Plantation—or Away Down South in Dixie," which purportedly showed "the most realistic sketch of Negro life in the South before the war." It did so by featuring singing, "cotton field frolics" and the Virginia reel.

By 1883, Mack's ability to perform and his life were in jeopardy. He fell ill with consumption, or tuberculosis. While in Cincinnati in April 1883, Mack was so ill that he was unable to leave his hotel room to perform. The newspapers ran the story under the headline "A Dying Rooster."[226] He was noted to be in the final stages of consumption, but he did manage to do a couple of performances in that engagement. Illness caused him to withdraw from performances in other cities during the year, as well.

Less than a month later, Mack was back at work. A reviewer in Jamestown, New York, described his act: "screamingly funny and kept the audience roaring with laughter. Mack's personation [*sic*] of an overgrown rooster is the best thing of the kind we have ever seen."[227] Another noted that "Bob Mack does the rooster act in a way that makes people hold on their sides."[228] By

1884, his son Little Bob Mack also made a name for himself. The three-year-old was billed as "the youngest and funniest comedian upon the stage."[229]

Despite his brief recoveries, Mack's illness ultimately became too much for him to continue. He died from consumption in Elmira on January 21, 1885, at the age of thirty-five. He was eulogized in obituaries in newspapers throughout the country. One noted, "Bob was a versatile man and had hosts of friends throughout the country."[230] Bob Mack's life and career were cut short, but he influenced performers who came after him. Others tried to replicate his chicken acts, but none could succeed as well as Mack. Decades later, Bert Williams did a version of the rooster performance in the Ziegfeld Follies.[231]

16

JOHN LAWES AND CHARLES BRADLEY

Freak shows" were popular forms of entertainment in Elmira and throughout America in the late nineteenth and early twentieth centuries. The people employed by the shows typically had some kind of physical difference or disability. While freak show and dime museum operators like P.T. Barnum could make a fortune, it often came through the exploitation of their "exhibits." Two Elmirans, John Lawes and Charles Bradley, found themselves singled out for their unique physiques, whether they wanted it or not.

John Lawes was an English immigrant and a blacksmith who lived in Elmira with his family. He garnered little public attention until the mid-1880s, when he began gaining weight at an alarming rate. Lawes, five feet, eight inches tall, normally weighed around 200 pounds, but by 1888, he reportedly weighed 440 pounds. He supposedly gained about two pounds a week.[232]

He tried in vain to lose weight, attempting "everyway possible to keep down his flesh. He worked hard, early and late, and even went on a diet, but it seemed to do no good for the flesh did not reduce. He became fatter and fatter until he gave up in despair."[233] As his weight increased, so did his appetite. The local newspapers sensationally reported that "two or three pounds of beefsteak was the merest 'snack' to him…he spent most of his time eating."[234] As his condition worsened, Lawes had to give up his work as a blacksmith, since he could no longer walk or move freely on his own. His weight peaked at 640 pounds.

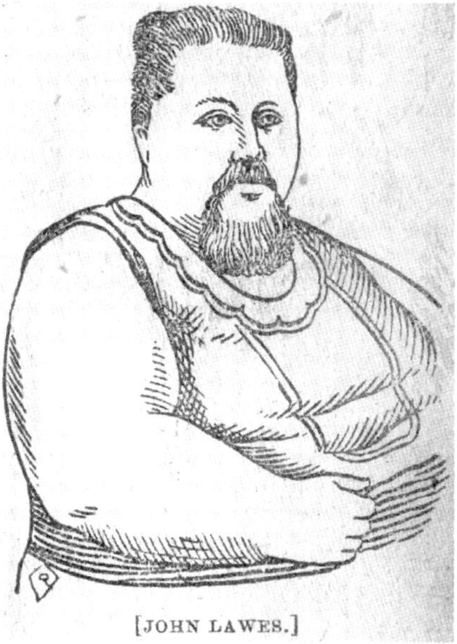

Drawing of John Lawes.

It was in this state that Lawes was approached by the manager of Barnum's dime museum. To the unemployed Lawes, the weekly salary of thirty-five dollars was too much to refuse. He toured in New York City and Philadelphia before returning to Elmira in June 1889 to do a stint at the Chemung County Fair.[235] Lawes died on June 17, 1889. The forty-year-old's condition had been so poor that one newspaper reported: "Under the circumstances it would seem as if death must have been a relief. Still, the huge man was of the happiest, best natured disposition in the world. He positively enjoyed showing his immense proportions to the admiring beholders."[236]

Some reports claimed he died from erysipelas, a skin infection, but he may have asphyxiated in bed in his home on Hart Street. Newspapers throughout the country ran a series of appalling headlines announcing his death, including "Heaviest Corpse On Earth," "Elmira's Heavy Loss" and "The Fat Man's Funeral." The funeral arrangements were printed in great detail. A special coffin had to be built, and from eight to twelve pallbearers were required. A crowd of onlookers trying to catch a glimpse of the dead man formed on the Lawes family's lawn. The coffin was so large that a carpenter had to be called to cut away part of the door frame and wall to fit it through. Lawes was buried in Woodlawn Cemetery in "a grave that looked like a cellar" while his widow and children wept.[237]

The Lawes family soldiered on after the loss of their patriarch. Son Harry L. Lawes became a respected Elmira police detective. Yet, for years, Elmirans remained morbidly fascinated with "Big John Lawes." In 1913, the Elmira Camera Club collected photographs of "old Elmira," and it proudly announced that it already had a photograph of "John Lawes sitting on two chairs."[238]

A couple of decades after Lawes's death, another local man, Charles Bradley, found fame for his unusual body. At points during his life, Bradley was reported to be the tallest man in the world, although this was likely untrue. Reports of his height varied between seven feet, four inches and seven feet, seven inches. Bradley was born into a family of tall people in Antrim, Pennsylvania, in 1890; his father was six feet, nine inches tall, and his siblings were all over six feet tall.

The Bradley family farmed in several towns in rural Steuben County, New York, throughout Charles's childhood. His rapid growth, however, made it difficult for Charles to help with the manual labor on the farm.[239] He and his family had already rejected several offers to display the boy in sideshows by the time he finally accepted a job with the Barnum & Bailey Circus in 1909. He was already seven feet, two inches tall.[240] The circus billed him as the "Tallest Boy in the World" and exhibited him next to the "World's Smallest Woman." Adding to the indignity of the proceedings, Bradley had to wear a Little Lord Fauntleroy costume. Such suits were only worn by young boys, and this outfit must have been humiliating for the nineteen-year-old Bradley.

Despite the fact that Bradley consented to being displayed, it was probably not without significant reservations. The language used in newspaper accounts of his hiring suggests he may have been an unwilling participant who "submitted to becoming an exhibit." Bradley was reportedly "turned over to the managers of the New York office of the Barnum & Bailey shows."[241] Perhaps the burden of not being able to fully work on the family farm led him to decide to contribute in this way.

In 1911, Bradley found work traveling around the country and dressing as Uncle Sam to promote Union Leader tobacco. In New Ulm, Minnesota, the Grand Hotel had to give its tall guest a bed that was open at the foot. The local newspaper marveled that the "human beanpole" wore size fourteen shoes. After an engagement in the local cigar store, he left for visits in Mankato and Waseca, Minnesota.[242]

Bradley left show business by the 1920s, when "he got tired of the life" and chose to follow "industrial pursuits."[243] He returned to the Southern Tier, taking up residence in Corning, Elmira and Elmira Heights. Bradley found work in factories and as a truck driver. He did still get occasional recognition for his height, however. He was reportedly the world's tallest member of the Loyal Order of the Moose. In the organization's parades, he marched with Elmira's Marguerite Morgan, who, at forty inches tall, was the smallest Mooseheart.[244] Other than those mentions, Bradley fell into obscurity, which seems to be what he wanted all along.

17

PROFESSOR SMOKEBALL

In the early 1900s, Godfrey Beirweiller, a German immigrant, became an unlikely local laughingstock. Beirweiller was better known to Elmirans as Professor Smokeball. He earned his nickname because he sold "smokeballs," or cloth balls of carbolic acid that supposedly cured illness. Beirweiller gained local infamy when, around 1903, he began giving spontaneous and amateur phrenology lectures and demonstrations that were more entertainment than science. Local newspapers reported on and mocked his every move. Records suggest that Beirweiller probably struggled with mental illness and addiction, and it is unclear to what degree he was in on the joke.

In early 1903, Beirweiller worked at Elmira's Hotel Rathbun, but little other information is available on his life before he became the self-proclaimed "Champion Phrenologist and Physiognomist of the World."[245] He claimed that he could use his past experiences to help the unwell, stating: "It is not necessary for anyone to go to an insane asylum. I can treat them just as well. I spent three years in the hospital for the insane in Warren, Pennsylvania, and I know how they took care of me, and can do the same for others."[246] He first drew attention for his beliefs and lectures at a 1903 Masonic Street Fair, parlaying the attention he received into other speaking engagements, both invited and not. He peddled his smokeballs with sales pitches such as the following: "This iss the zeason uf the year ven vrightful kuffs and kulds uppear, und then the dread kunzumpshun kums und dakes the zuffering shildren hum. Browngitus, groop und whooping golf, they zure do dake the shildren off; shout Its praises vide und var, Garbollc Smokeballs gure guitar."[247]

By the end of 1903 and the start of 1904, Beirweiller gave lectures around the region with increasing frequency. In September 1903, "The walls of the assembly chamber of the city hall echoed" with Beirweiller's proselytizing for the "benefit of the office force of policemen at headquarters, the janitors, the various clerk, and a few others."[248] Beirweiller offered to read strangers' heads, and he also introduced his "tree of life" chart into his impromptu lessons.

Within just a few years, Beirweiller's nickname became a popularly recognized slur for anyone doing anything stupid or self-aggrandizing. When a boxer had a meltdown in the ring, it was reported that "In a Professor Smokeball attitude, he announced to the 'gents' from the ring that he was a professional, and not a 'hamacher' boxer."[249] Another man was described as "the butt of many jokes as 'Professor Smokeballs' is now."[250] Beirweiller was keenly aware that he was the target of jokes and pranks. When he was invited to give a lecture at Park Church in 1908, he said he would only do it "providing no one puts eggs in his pocket or sodium in his beer."[251]

Beirweiller frequently found himself in trouble with the law. On March 31, 1908, Elmira chief of police Frank Cassada arrested him for illegally soliciting business and told him to leave the city within an hour or face charges.[252] At that point, Beirweiller relocated to a farm near Horseheads. It was reported, however, that "his rural employer did not take kindly to his lectures and insisted upon work instead of talk....Despite the fact that it is the 'professor's' contention that a healthy man can talk at least eleven hours a day without fatigue or strain, he was not allowed to peep a word when the boss of the farm was about."[253] Beirweiller longed to be back in Elmira and continuing his practice. He said he was looking for a manager or press agent and announced his intention to raise the money necessary to attend a phrenology conference in New York City.[254]

He slowly added to his conference travel fund, making $1.25 in twenty minutes speaking at a Shriners banquet.[255] His efforts were derailed when, in May 1908, he was robbed of thirty-five pennies while he was sleeping. Beirweiller reported the crime to the police and called every two hours for updates on the case. The police, clearly becoming less amused by the relatively trivial case every time Beirweiller checked in, claimed they were "working with all their influence to fathom the mystery."[256] Shortly after, he was arrested for drunkenness—neither the first nor the last time he faced that charge.

Despite his setbacks, Beirweiller made his way to New York City by foot that fall. He was arrested in Brooklyn on September 30, 1908, for intoxication. He claimed to be a professor of phrenology with a Manhattan office, which turned out to be a room in a boardinghouse. The "seedily dressed man, bearing a generally soiled appearance" told the judge he was not drunk, explaining instead:

> *It's just this way, your honor....I must keep talking in order to remain awake, but the minute I stop I fall asleep. I entered the saloon for a glass of beer, and, as a pastime, read the head of the bartender, who in turn insisted on giving me whisky. Immediately after that I fell into a profound slumber.*[257]

In June 1909, Beirweiller returned to Elmira, where he resumed lecturing, this time also performing an original song, "I May Be Crazy, But I Get the Money."[258] In July 1911, he was twice arrested for intoxication. The first time, he was drunk in Wisner Park and was brought to the county jail, where "the unfortunate ones who had never heard the professor give his crazy lingo were entertained until late at night."[259] When he was arrested again, on July 25, he was sent out of town by the police. Beirweiller spun this, claiming he was leaving on another "lecture tour."[260] He sent letters back to the local newspapers while on "tour" in other regional cities. In the letters, Beirweiller played into his reputation, once stating, "I know a great many of the subscribers of Elmira newspapers informed me that they always look up the Professor Smokeball news first of all others."[261]

Beirweiller continued to make local news through at least 1916. Throughout his career, people debated whether Beirweiller knew that people were laughing at him and not with him. In some ways, it appears that he consciously embraced his role as a community entertainer. In one of the final notices of a return visit to Elmira, the reporter noted: "Everyone kids the professor yet all of the time the professor is kidding everybody else. He is one of those fellows who makes a living by letting people kid him."[262]

18

THE WONDERFUL WELSH BROTHERS

The Welsh brothers were arguably the most famous Elmira family that no one remembers. In the late nineteenth and early twentieth centuries, Thomas, Joseph and William not only were popular locally, but each also gained national or international acclaim for their theatrical exploits. The three brothers were born to Grafton, a teacher, and Elizabeth Welsh. They had a half-sister, Eliza Lattimer, from Elizabeth's first marriage, who was a locally recognized concerto singer in her youth.

Thomas Grant Welsh, the middle brother, was born in 1872 and came of age in the golden age of roller skating. A roller-skating craze took hold of America in the 1880s, and Elmira was no exception. Roller rinks were built throughout the city, and Elmirans of all ages skated and were spectators for exhibitions of trick and fancy skating. By 1885, Harry Curtis, owner of Elmira's Mascot Rink, put together three teams of young trick skaters that toured the country. Young Tom Welsh, who displayed a great talent for skating, was paired with another local boy, Joe Powell, to form the team Powell and Welsh.[263] Touted as the "Champion Boy Skaters," they were reported to "have acquired a splendid reputation. Their exhibitions are said to be something out of the usual line and very entertaining."[264] They toured in New York, Pennsylvania, Ohio and West Virginia. Thomas quit his professional roller-skating career by the 1890s, but he did give one final exhibition performance in 1905 at Elmira's Casino Rink. Despite the long gap since his skating fame, he reportedly had "lost none of his agility since that time." The display was met with much praise.[265]

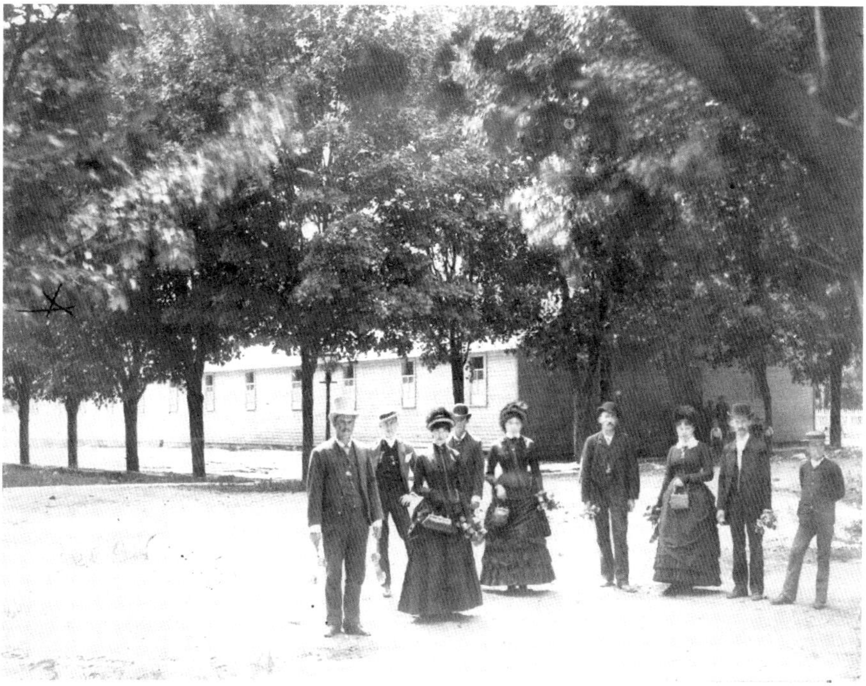

Roller skaters in Elmira in 1885, the same year Thomas Welsh began touring as a trick skater.

By the 1890s, Thomas became a barber and set up shops in Athens, Pennsylvania and Elmira. He eventually was appointed barber inspector for Chemung County, and in 1905, he became president of the Elmira Barbers' Association and vice president of the New York State Barbers' Association.[266] Thomas's work in the local and state barbers' organizations paved the way for him to be more involved with labor concerns. He parlayed his reputation as "one of the most popular young men of the city" to run for president of the local assembly of the Federation of Labor.[267]

Thomas made a name for himself in local politics and became a city supervisor by the early 1900s. In 1906, while serving as supervisor of the sixth district, he caused "a sensation" when he called for specifications regarding the repair of county buildings in an attempt to uncover graft.[268] Other senior supervisors blocked his efforts, saying he was "playing to the grand stand."[269] In the 1920s, when he was serving as county election commissioner, there were rumors he would run for Congress. But he never did. He ultimately relocated to Brooklyn around 1940 and died there of a heart ailment on October 30, 1945.

The youngest brother, Joseph Scott Welsh, was born on December 7, 1875, and became a renowned tenor and actor. His first theater appearance was as part of a group of children in a picnic scene in *Edgewood Folks* at the Elmira Opera House.[270] Elmirans noticed his talent early on; while he was still in school, the newspapers remarked:

> *Mr. Welsh has a voice of great sweetness and power and he uses it without apparent effort....It is a voice that entrances and lingers in the memory like the heroics of speech and the tone of deep feeling. It has been said that Italians were the only people in the world who could sing, but Mr. Welsh's voice is the singing voice that can vocalize our beautiful English language. In fact, Mr. Welsh was an Apollo in knee breeches.*[271]

Local theater critic Platt V. Bryan paid Joseph this strange compliment: "Mr. J.S. Welsh has a voice sweet enough for a girl, and we are always delighted to hear it." After graduation, he worked as an engraver for the *Elmira Telegram* newspaper, but it was joked that "he was 'scooped' so many times he decided to be an actor."[272]

Joseph left Elmira for New York City around 1900. Soon after, he changed his stage name to Scott Welsh to distinguish himself from another acting Joseph Welsh.[273] He was cast in several shows that toured the East Coast and began to gain widespread acclaim. Joseph married actress Frances Gordon on August 15, 1906. Joseph and Frances were a theatrical power couple, often starring in the same show and touring together. In the summer of 1909, the pair even relaxed in style, renting a cottage in Cohasset, Massachusetts, where they cruised on a motorboat.

In 1909, Joseph joined the cast of the play *The Man Who Owned Broadway*, his first Broadway show. Frances was also in the show, playing his love interest. Joseph acted in six more Broadway plays throughout his career: *Oh! Oh! Delphine* (1912–13), *Eileen* (1917), *She's a Good Fellow* (1919), *Tip Top* (1920–21), *Princess Ida* (1925) and *A Play Without a Name* (1928–29). In between these engagements, Joseph maintained a busy schedule of other touring shows.

Even as his professional stature grew, Joseph always made time to come back to Elmira to perform. As the *Elmira Star-Gazette* put it, "and through it all Scott is wearing the same sized hat."[274] Joseph relished his time back in Elmira, saying, "I'm going home to the town and the people I love the most in all the world, where I was a boy and turned handsprings in the tanbark with my brothers, Tom and Bill."[275] For years, Joseph returned to star in the summer operas at Rorick's Glen.

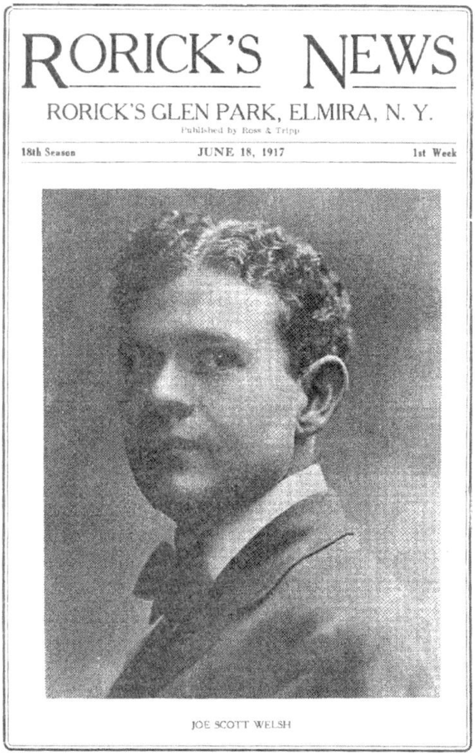

RORICK'S NEWS

RORICK'S GLEN PARK, ELMIRA, N. Y.

Published by Ross & Tripp

18th Season JUNE 18, 1917 1st Week

JOE SCOTT WELSH

Right: A program for hometown favorite Joe Scott Welsh's performance at Rorick's Glen in 1917.

Below: Joe Scott Welsh (in tuxedo, at center of the second row from the bottom) with the opera company at Rorick's Glen, 1916.

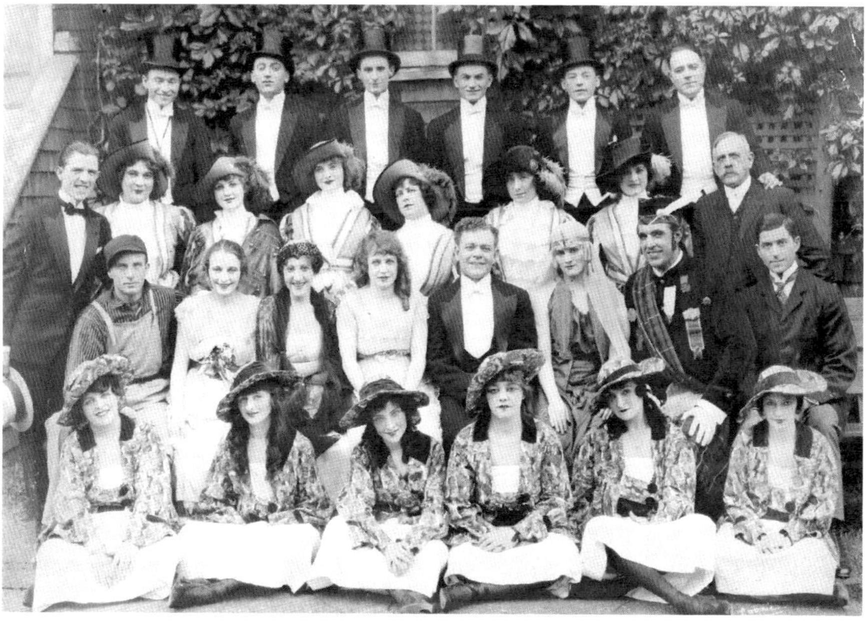

The local audiences and press fawned over his performances and dedication to the city. The end of the 1916 Rorick's season inspired the following reaction:

> *He grows on us year by year, and is ever a revelation, for there is to his personality charm, grace and a pleasing individuality. It is with such words tribute is generally paid to a prima donna, but this time they apply to Joe Welsh. We know him as a wholesome young man, particular about the best things in life and ardent in their practice. He is of the salt of the earth. His voice has a resonance of rare value. His enunciation is distinct and sharp but not harsh. Its traveling qualities are marvelous.... There was a grand demonstration for the Elmiran as he sang songs denoting his love for the "old home town." The company entered into the spirit of the evening and sang him "Good Bye Scott!"*[276]

Joseph also returned in 1917 to perform in a vaudeville and carnival fundraiser for Elmira's Ambulance Corps.[277]

Tragedy struck on July 14, 1921, when Frances jumped from a window of their third-story room at the Carleton Hotel in Atlantic City, New Jersey. Joseph was in the room getting dressed and only discovered that something was wrong when he heard her scream. She died from a skull fracture minutes after arriving at the hospital. The couple had come to Atlantic City five weeks earlier in the hopes of easing the symptoms of Frances's long illness. She was supposedly recovering, and the *New York Times* called her suicide a "temporary mental derangement."[278] The *New-York Tribune* printed a brief death notice stating only that the "beloved wife of Scott Welsh" died and that her interment would be private.[279]

Despite his grief, Joseph continued his busy schedule. In the 1920s, he entered the newly burgeoning film industry. He had parts in three silent films: *Bits of Life* (1921), which featured Chinese American Hollywood pioneer Anna May Wong; *Wild Oats Lane* (1926); and *Whispering Wires* (1926). In local advertisements for the films, the credit "An Elmira Boy" was added under Joseph's name. He was apparently typecast a bit: he played a detective in all three movies.[280]

He continued working until at least the late 1920s. Joseph died at Fifth Avenue Hospital in New York City on April 19, 1931, after a long illness. He was buried with his wife in Westchester County. He was remembered as being "a light hearted fellow, of a happy disposition, who always had a smile and a kindly word of greeting."[281]

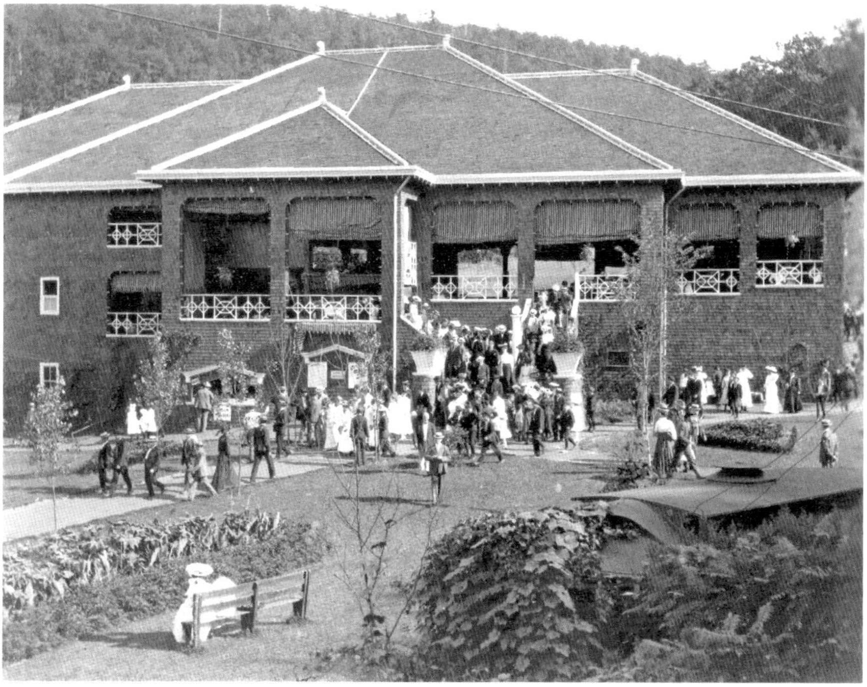

The Rorick's Glen Theater.

Firstborn William Lincoln Welsh was the most famous of his well-known siblings. Born in 1867, he went on to form one half of the husband-wife contortionist, juggling and acting duo De Hollis and Valora. William took the stage name De Hollis while working as a solo performer with various circuses in the 1880s. While his reasons for choosing this name in particular have been lost to history, the name change was necessitated to distinguish himself from the two other unrelated Welshes on the staff of one of his first circuses. When William married Josephine Valliard in 1890, the pair adopted the stage names De Hollis and Valora.

De Hollis and Valora's work took them far away from Elmira as they joined various vaudeville troops throughout the 1890s and early 1900s. They toured extensively in the United States and around the world. Their grueling international travel schedule kept William and Josephine away from home most of the time. When they were in town, it was cause for celebration, and they gave performances in Elmira, honoring their original fan base. They were often billed as "comic jugglers," and William gained a reputation for juggling odd objects. He was known for "playfully allowing a cannon ball to come within an ace of his skull."[282] The duo's plate juggling was said to be "sparklingly funny, and compelled even the joke-soaked orchestra to glue to it on several sequential nights."[283] Another trick inspired some playful sabotage by theater workers in Alton, Illinois, much to William's dismay. One trick in William's arsenal involved him using a fork held in his mouth to catch an apple thrown from a balcony. For several performances, the theater boys tasked with tossing the apple thought it funny to take a bite out of it before throwing it to the stage. William had his revenge at another performance, however, when he drilled holes in the apple and filled them with hot pepper.[284]

Josephine, though mentioned less frequently in the press, was vital to the success of the acts, and she possessed skills William did not. She was an accomplished singer and actress. When touring with the Hunting Circus, it was reported, "Mrs. De Hollis is a great hit with this season and now devotes nearly all her time to the concert, taking a leading part."[285] When she took a part in an Elmira staging of *Pocahontas*, she was praised for her "delicate sleight-of-hand performance."[286]

As their fame grew, De Hollis and Valora spent more time out of the country. By the end of their careers, they had performed in North and South America, Europe, Asia and Australia. In the early 1910s, they joined the Great Jansen Show to perform in its world tour, and William also served as the manager of the show. Elmira and trade newspapers reprinted anecdotes and letters the pair sent home. The letters reveal their exploits as they spent months traveling by boat and performing in places like Hawaii, Japan, China, the Philippines and Australia.[287] The most amusing story came from their stay in China. After completing a successful private performance for a Chinese potentate and his daughter in Peking, an interpreter told William that the princess had decided to marry him and wanted to know when he would be ready. William had to politely decline her proposal, explaining that he "already had one wife." Not easily deterred, the princess followed the show to Shanghai and requested to appear in William's juggling act. He joked: "You see the princess was particularly interested in the trick where I catch the cannon ball on the back of my neck. Perhaps she thought she might some day see my head fly off my body. I believe that would have pleased her."[288]

William relayed another humorous incident from Java, Indonesia. While performing in the sultan's palace, which was hung on all sides with silk curtains, he noticed that the walls were whispering. He discovered

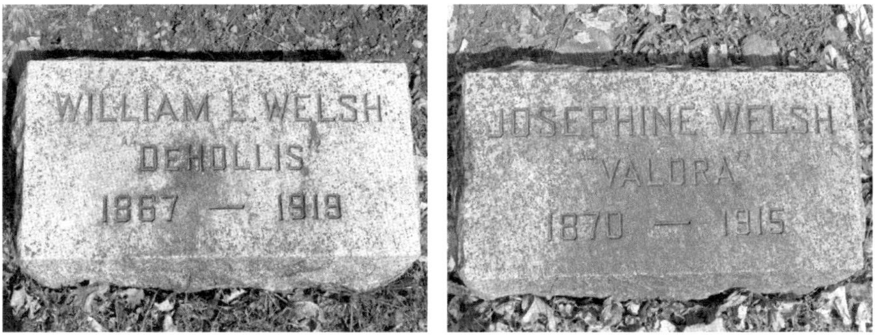

The graves of William and Josephine Welsh in Woodlawn Cemetery. Their stage names are engraved on their headstones. *Photographs by author.*

that the sultan's entire harem of three hundred women was hiding behind the curtains, watching the performance.

Sometime during that trip or on their return from Australia in 1913, however, Josephine fell ill. Her illness was never identified in the press; it was reported that she had been injured in their act, but that may not have been true. The pair returned to Elmira for her recovery. Josephine was unable to return to the stage with her husband, so he began performing alone. While performing in Indianapolis in 1915, William received a telegram that his wife had died in Elmira.

William continued to perform after Josephine's death. He hired an assistant and toured South America. He died in Buenos Aires, Argentina, in 1919. His body was shipped back to his family in Elmira and was buried in Woodlawn Cemetery next to his wife. Like the true performers they were, both William and Josephine have their stage names engraved on their headstones.

Neither William nor Joseph had any children. Thomas's first daughter, Rosemary, died as a baby, and his other daughter, Hazel, never married. The family line of the talented Welsh brothers ended when Hazel died in Denver, Colorado, in 1981.

CONCLUSION

Elmira's past is brimming with far more colorful characters than could possibly fit within the pages of this book. In fact, whittling down the list to just the few people and stories included here was a painstaking process. We are constantly discovering new people, events and sources that add richness to our ever-expanding understanding of our collective local past. This book was originally supposed to be a lighthearted look at the past, and in many ways, it is. There is a lot of humor in some of these stories, especially in the ways that the press discussed them. But when the stories were fully researched and committed to paper, they revealed more complexity. Although these stories are "curiosities" that, for the most part, took place well over one hundred years ago, they are still deeply and recognizably human tales of joy, experimentation and fun—but also of loss, illness and tragedy. That is what makes it so compelling to research and write these stories.

When I work with students, they often have trouble reconciling the fact that people in the past, born decades or centuries before them, faced the same range of emotions and experiences they do. In many ways, history can be abstract, and chronological distance lulls us into the idea that people were somehow fundamentally different or less human than we are today. I make it one of my missions to help re-"humanize" historical figures when I teach, and I hope that I have done the same in this book.

NOTES

Chapter 1

1. "A Wonderful Invention," *Weekly Standard*, January 10, 1866.
2. *Circular of the American Aelloscope Company*, 15.
3. Ibid., vi.
4. Ibid., 29.
5. "The French Exposition," *New York Times*, July 30, 1867, 2.
6. "Philosophical Instruments at the Paris Exhibition," *Gentleman's Magazine*, November 1867, 662.
7. "Aerial Navigation," *Addison Advertiser*, July 1, 1875.

Chapter 2

8. "How Elmira Became the World's Largest Fire Apparatus Manufacturing Center," Chemung County Historical Society.
9. *Elmira Star-Gazette*, November 16, 1914, 9.
10. "The Ancient Asa La France Band," *Elmira Telegram*, December 24, 1916.
11. Ibid.
12. "My Last Tribute to Asa La France," *Elmira Telegram*, December 21, 1916.
13. "That Old La France Band Again," *Elmira Telegram*, January 21, 1917.
14. "The La France Steamer," *Tri-State Union*, May 4, 1877.

15. "New La France Fire Engine," *Elmira Telegram*, January 11, 1891.
16. "A Well-Known Man," *Elmira Daily Gazette and Free Press*, September 16, 1895, 5.
17. "Inventions of Mr. La France," *Elmira Gazette and Free Press*, March 30, 1904.
18. "Messrs. La France and Moore Leave," *Elmira Gazette and Free Press*, July 22, 1905.
19. "Beachey Accepts Challenge of LaFrance Motor Car Co.," *Elmira Star-Gazette*, July 25, 1911.
20. "Fire Engine Company Formally Dissolves," *Elmira Star-Gazette*, June 18, 1914, 14.
21. "Asa LaFrance," *Elmira Telegram*, May 7, 1916.
22. "Asa La France Retires," *Elmira Telegram*, March 19, 1916.

Chapter 3

23. "The Philo System Investigated," *Reliable Poultry Journal* 16, no. 11 (January 1910): 1,240.
24. *Troy Daily Times*, March 16, 1887.
25. *Elmira Star-Gazette*, March 16, 1910, 7.
26. Philo, *Philo System*, 3.
27. Ibid., 39.
28. Ibid.
29. "The Philo System Investigated," *Reliable Poultry Journal* 16, no. 1 (December 1909): 1,050.
30. John F. Graham, "The Business End of the Poultry Business," *Annual Report of the Secretary of the Connecticut Board of Agriculture*, 1912, 138–39.
31. *Pacific Coast Fancier's Monthly* 19, no. 3 (March, 1909): 80.
32. Charles Weeks, "The Most Intensive Egg Farm in the World," *American Poultry Journal* 49 (1918): 548.
33. "The Philo System Investigated," *Reliable Poultry Journal* 16, no. 11 (January 1910): 1,240.

Chapter 4

34. The Hungerfords' story has been covered in great detail in the following works: Geoffrey N. Stein, *Daniel and Floyd Hungerford: Rocket Power, Interstellar Travel and Eternal Life*; Keith Marvin, "The Wizards of West Second

Street" and "Misguided Missile"; Igor Spajic, "The Hungerford Rocket Car"; Peg Gallagher, "Moonstruck"; and others.

35. "Bleriot Monoplane Arrives in Elmira," *Elmira Star-Gazette*, August 21, 1913, 11.
36. "Elmiran in Aeroplane He Has Built Soon May Be Flying Over the City," *Elmira Star-Gazette*, May 6, 1914, 12.
37. "Elmirans Get New Airplane," *Elmira Star-Gazette,* April 18, 1917, 14.
38. "Would Form Air Chapter," *Elmira Star-Gazette*, August 6, 1923, 17.
39. "Soon Hold Contest to Promote Interest in Aircraft Building," *Elmira Star-Gazette*, March 31, 1924, 16.
40. "Supervisors of Playgrounds Hear Talk on Model Airplanes," *Elmira Star-Gazette*, July 19, 1927, 3.
41. "Boy Students Repair Planes," *Elmira Star-Gazette*, August 11, 1927, 14.
42. "Hungerfords Get License Friday for County's First Rocket Car," *Elmira Star-Gazette*, August 15, 1931, 2.
43. "18,000 Marchers Greeted Joyfully as Jubilee Reigns," *Elmira Star-Gazette*, 1933.

Chapter 5

44. "Cleveland's Queer Boom," *Amsterdam Daily Democrat*, October 20, 1884.
45. "Pardon Crazy," *Buffalo Express*, October 21, 1884, 1.
46. Hilpert, *American Cyclone.*
47. "Work of Boys," *Elmira Daily Gazette and Free Press*, November 3, 1900.
48. "Corning Boys Fared Badly," *Elmira Daily Gazette and Free Press*, October 30, 1900.
49. "Bryanism Blamed for Rowdyism," *New York Press*, October 31, 1900.
50. "Corning's Hearty Welcome," *Gloversville Daily Leader*, October 30, 1900, 1.
51. *Port Jervis Tri-States Union*, November 1, 1900.
52. "Bryanism Rampant," *New-York Daily Tribune*, November 2, 1900.
53. "Many Regrets Are Expressed," *Elmira Daily Gazette and Free Press*, October 30, 1900.
54. "The Elmira Disturbance," *New York Times*, October 31, 1900, 5.
55. "Crime Rampant," *Elmira Daily Gazette and Free Press*, October 30, 1900.
56. "Chief Cassada Talks," *Elmira Daily Gazette and Free Press*, October 31, 1900.
57. "Reward Is Offered," *Elmira Daily Gazette and Free Press*, November 1, 1900.

58. "Police Board Held Meeting," *Elmira Daily Gazette and Free Press*, November 2, 1900.
59. Elmiran John Stanchfield was running for Roosevelt's soon-to-be vacant governor position. "Work of Boys," *Elmira Daily Gazette and Free Press*, November 3, 1900.

Chapter 6

60. "Miss Ella White's Doings," *Elmira Telegram*, April 7, 1889, 4.
61. "Pretty, But a Stock Gambler," *New York Press*, April, 10, 1889, 8.
62. *Owego Record*, January 9, 1890.
63. "Ella White's Escape," *Elmira Telegram*, January 12, 1890, 8.
64. "Ella White Breaks Jail," *Elmira Telegram*, January 12, 1890, 5.
65. *Havana Journal*, January 18, 1890.
66. "Was She Ella White?," *Elmira Telegram*, May 25, 1890, 8.
67. "Ella White Scandalized," *Elmira Telegram*, February 8, 1891.
68. "Chief Little Back," *Elmira Daily Gazette and Free Press*, May 9, 1892, 7.
69. "It Creates a Smile," *Elmira Daily Gazette and Free Press*, May 7, 1892, 5.
70. "Mysteries Are Solved," *Elmira Daily Gazette and Free Press*, June 6, 1899.
71. "Killed Her Paramour," *Port Jervis Evening Gazette*, January 11, 1890.
72. "'Bill Edwards's Fate," *Albany Express*, January 11, 1890.
73. "Murder in Elmira," *Elmira Telegram*, January 12, 1890.
74. *Havana Journal*, January 18, 1890.
75. *Waverly Free Press*, May 31, 1890.
76. "A Noted Murder Trial," *Watkins Express*, October 23, 1890.
77. "Is Not Guilty!," *Elmira Telegram*, October 19, 1890, 7.
78. Ibid.
79. "T.K. Beecher's Position," *Elmira Telegram*, October 26, 1890, 4; "Mr. Beecher's Position," *Elmira Telegram*, November 2, 1890, 4.
80. "Assaulted His Mother," *Elmira Daily Gazette and Free Press*, November 17, 1891, 5.
81. "No Confession," *Elmira Daily Gazette and Free Press*, August 26, 1893.
82. "Mrs. Mary Eilenburger Dead," *Elmira Telegram*, August 20, 1893.
83. "Ada's Escape," *Brooklyn Daily Eagle*, June 25, 1886, 6.
84. "Pretty Ada Hull's Story," *New York Sun*, June 25, 1886, 1.
85. "The Runaways," *Brooklyn Union*, July 11, 1886, 2.
86. "Mrs. Mattie Barber a Free Woman," *Elmira Telegram*, September 14, 1890, 6.

87. "Court News of the Week," *Elmira Telegram*, March 23, 1890, 8.
88. "A New York Paper Sued," *Elmira Telegram*, January 11, 1891, 5.

Chapter 7

89. "Christmas Gifts," *Elmira Telegram*, December 27, 1891, 6.
90. "Comstock's Lively Raid," *Elmira Telegram*, November 19, 1893, 4.
91. "Gilmore's Examination," *Elmira Daily Gazette and Free Press*, November 18, 1893.
92. "Comstock in Elmira," *Elmira Daily Gazette and Free Press*, November 18, 1893, 4.
93. "Comstock's Lively Raid," 4.
94. Ibid.
95. "Gilmore Was Indicted," *Elmira Daily Gazette and Free Press*, November 23, 1893, 7.
96. "Looking Hopeful for Lew Gilmore," *Elmira Telegram*, December 24, 1893.
97. "Causes a Smile," *Elmira Daily Gazette and Free Press*, January 23, 1894, 3.
98. "Had a Big Time," *Elmira Daily Gazette and Free Press*, November 30, 1894, 5.
99. *Deruyter Gleaner*, January 3, 1895.
100. "Why Elmirans Would Enlist," *Elmira Daily Gazette and Free Press*, March 2, 1898, 6.
101. "'Blue Front' Is a Wreck," *Elmira Daily Gazette and Free Press*, March 7, 1898.
102. "'Lew' Gilmore," *Elmira Telegram*, October 3, 1915.

Chapter 8

103. *Watkins Express*, February 13, 1879.
104. Ibid.
105. "The Fire at Elmira on Sunday Morning," *New York Times*, December 28, 1866.
106. *Corning Journal*, September 2, 1869.
107. "The Taghanic Fraud," *Hornellsville Tribune*, July 25, 1879.
108. *Steuben Courier*, April 3, 1872.
109. "Harry Beadle, of Elmira," *New York Times*, May 12, 1878.

110. *Watkins Democrat*, May 1, 1878.
111. "The Bank of Chemung Investigation," *New York Times*, April 13, 1878.
112. *Watkins Democrat*, September 25, 1878.
113. Gregg, *Revised Catalogue*, 23.
114. *Bulletin of the Nuttall Ornithologial Club* 5, no. 3 (July 1880): 173.
115. Dutcher, *Labrador Duck*, 215.
116. *Corning Journal*, May 4, 1882.

Chapter 9

117. "Figures Presented," *Elmira Daily Gazette and Free Press*, July 26, 1892, 6.
118. "The Famous Bear Pit," *Elmira Telegram*, July 26, 1891, 8.
119. "Pennsylvanians Picnic," *Elmira Daily Gazette and Free Press*, August 28, 1891, 7.
120. "That Bear Pit Again," *Elmira Telegram*, September 1893, 8.
121. "Bruin Didn't Like It," *Elmira Daily Gazette and Free Press*, July 5, 1892, 7.
122. "Torture Animals in Eldridge Park," *Elmira Star-Gazette*, July 9, 1909, 12.
123. "Where Summer Pets Spend Long Winter," *Elmira Daily Gazette and Free Press*, December 29, 1903.
124. "No Hibernating for Tessie; Eldridge Park 'Zoo' Leaves That for Uncivilized Bears," *Elmira Star-Gazette*, March 12, 1930, 24.
125. "Big Bear Fight," *Elmira Daily Gazette and Free Press*, August 19, 1895, 7.
126. "Big Bear Killed Little One," *Elmira Daily Gazette and Free Press*, October 21, 1903.
127. "Big Bear Kills Cub," *Corning Journal*, October 28, 1903, 3.
128. "One Bear Gone," *Elmira Gazette and Free Press*, April 18, 1906.
129. "Eldridge Park Bear Is Killed," *Elmira Star-Gazette*, March 11, 1911, 7.
130. "Letters from the People," *Elmira Telegram*, June 4, 1905.
131. "That Park Bear Gets Out Again," *Elmira Star-Gazette*, January 8, 1909, 2.
132. "Will Hold Fair Sept. 16 to 20," *Elmira Star-Gazette*, February 3, 1912, 2.
133. "The New Bear Pit," *Elmira Star-Gazette*, July 29, 1912, 4.
134. "Trio of Cub Bears Here to Be Put in Eldridge," *Elmira Star-Gazette*, May 9, 1914, 11.
135. "Park's Old Bear Pit Becoming Roadway Now," *Elmira Star-Gazette*, April 5, 1940, 9.

Chapter 10

136. "Sea Lion Escaping," *Cortland Evening Standard*, June 23, 1903, 5.
137. "Sea Lion in Chenango River," *Auburn Argus*, June 24, 1903.
138. "Anxious Keeper of the Sea Lion," *Syracuse Journal*, June 27, 1903, 5.
139. *Rome Daily Sentinel*, July 2, 1903, 4.
140. *Genoa Tribune*, July 10, 1903, 1.
141. "Sea Lion in Chemung River," Chemung County Historical Society.
142. "A Sea Lion Found," *Cortland Standard*, July 28, 1903, 1.
143. "Sea Lion Is Dead," *Cortland Evening Standard*, July 27, 1903, 7.
144. "Seal Had Been in City Before," *Elmira Daily Gazette and Free Press*, July 27, 1903.
145. "Caused Excitement," *Elmira Telegram*, August 2, 1903.
146. "Has the Sea Lion," *Elmira Telegram*, August 2, 1903.
147. "Boone Plans Replevin Action to Get Body of His Sea Lion," *Syracuse Post Standard*, August 10, 1903.

Chapter 11

148. "Need Garbage Disposal," *Elmira Star-Gazette*, August 10, 1916, 6.
149. "A Tip for Elmira," *Elmira Star-Gazette*, August 8, 1917, 6.
150. "Is War Measure," *Elmira Star-Gazette*, August 15, 1918, 6.
151. "Do Not Favor Crematory," *Elmira Star-Gazette*, October 16, 1918, 6.
152. "Garbage Disposal," *Elmira Star-Gazette*, September 2, 1919, 6.
153. "Elmirans Will Establish New Piggery," *Elmira Star-Gazette*, August 30, 1919, 3.
154. "About the Piggery," *Elmira Star-Gazette*, September 13, 1919, 6.
155. "Shall We Feed $20,000 to Pigs," *Elmira Telegram*, September 14, 1919.
156. "Drake Piggery Plan Is Tabled by Board," *Elmira Star-Gazette*, September 24, 1919, 13.
157. "Drake Withdraws His Piggery Offer," *Elmira Star-Gazette*, September 27, 1919, 2.
158. "City Has No Plans in View to Set Up Municipal Piggery," *Elmira Star-Gazette*, October 1, 1919, 2.
159. "Wants to Know If He'll Take Piggery Stock," *Elmira Star-Gazette*, October 10, 1919, 11.
160. *Elmira Star-Gazette*, October 29, 1919, 16.
161. "Is Objection to Piggeries," *Elmira Star-Gazette*, March 7, 1922, 2.

162. "It Is Only Natural," *Elmira Star-Gazette*, March 24, 1922, 13.
163. *Elmira Star-Gazette*, May 3, 1922, 20.
164. "Rushing the Can Is Chief Pastime for Dealers Here," *Elmira Star-Gazette*, June 3, 1922, 9.
165. "Make Ready for Garbage Collections," *Elmira Star-Gazette*, May 12, 1922, 15.
166. "Investors May Lose $100,000 in Murphy Process Co. Report," *Corning Evening Leader*, February 14, 1923, 9.
167. "Southport Citizens Protest Against Proposed Piggery Farm," *Elmira Star-Gazette*, March 23, 1923, 24.
168. "More Complaints Are Made, Piggery Outside City Line," *Elmira Star-Gazette*, June 22, 1923, 16.
169. "Abandon Free Collections of Garbage for Old Plan," *Elmira Star-Gazette*, May 23, 1923.

Chapter 12

170. "A Sensation in Spiritualism," *Syracuse Daily Courier*, September 19, 1876.
171. *Corning Journal*, August 23, 1883.
172. *Geneva Courier*, August 6, 1873.
173. "Vienna Allen," *Biographical Record of Chemung County*, 153–54.
174. "Mrs. Vienna Allen," *Evening Leader*, March 6, 1920, 3.
175. "Family of Murdered Hornby Man Consult Clairvoyant in Elmira," *Elmira Star-Gazette*, June 20, 1919, 2.
176. "Mrs. Mary E. Stroman," *Elmira Star-Gazette*, April 2, 1924, 3.
177. *Schuyler County Democrat*, August 1871.
178. *Corning Journal*, September 11, 1890.
179. "First Spiritual Unity Society," *Biographical Record of Chemung County*, 429–30.
180. "Spiritualist New Pastor," *Elmira Daily Gazette and Free Press*, May 1, 1902.
181. "Comes Back at Father Van Allen," *Elmira Daily Gazette and Free Press*, May 23, 1902.
182. "Successful Treatment of Liver Disease," *Watkins Express*, August 24, 1893.
183. "A Successful Specialist," *Watkins Express*, October 12, 1893.
184. "A Modern Miracle," *Elmira Daily Gazette and Free Press*, February 13, 1893, 8.

185. "The Wonderful Magnetic Healer," *Naples Record,* April 13, 1892.
186. "After Dr. Frank Lyon," *Elmira Daily Gazette and Free Press*, November 25, 1893, 7.
187. "Prof. Frank Lyon," *Elmira Daily Gazette and Free Press,* December 22, 1893.
188. *Corning Journal,* October 31, 1879.
189. "Dr. I.C. Dow," *Corning Journal,* May 24, 1899, 5.
190. *Corning Journal,* August 24, 1882.
191. "He Works Wonders," *Elmira Daily Gazette and Free Press,* December 15, 1898, 7.
192. *Havana Journal,* January 9, 1875.
193. *Hornellsville Weekly Tribune,* November 26, 1880.
194. "Mayor 'Shows' Missourian Who Lectures On Phrenology," *Elmira Daily Gazette and Free Press,* June 27, 1907.

Chapter 13

195. "Young Boys Were Ghosts," *Elmira Gazette and Free Press*, September 28, 1905.
196. "Ghosts," *Elmira Daily Advertiser,* January 1, 1880.
197. "Elmira's Mysterious Lady," *Elmira Telegram,* June 3, 1888.
198. "Old Wilcox Hotel," *Elmira Daily Gazette and Free Press,* August 3, 1897, 3.
199. "Spook Is Seen in Grave Yard?," *Elmira Star-Gazette,* May 12, 1908, 2.
200. "Porter Declares Place Is Haunted," *Elmira Star-Gazette,* January 6, 1910, 4.

Chapter 14

201. "Miss Jenny Jewell's Readings," *Albany Atlas and Argus*, September 14, 1859. Italics in original.
202. Chemung County Historical Society, collection MC 79, Box A, folder 6; Thomas and Jeannie Jewell Hotchkiss collection, MC 72, Box A, folder 13.
203. *Williamsport Sun-Gazette*, November 8, 1875, 1.
204. *Medina Tribune*, December 5, 1878.
205. "An Elmira Belle Abroad," *Elmira Telegram*, April 10, 1892, 3.

206. *The Tennessean*, March 28, 1889, 2.
207. "Albany Notes," *Elmira Telegram*, July 8, 1894.
208. *Detroit Free Press*, May 18, 1889, 3.
209. Bessie Hotchkiss scrapbooks, SL:14:3 and SL:14:4, Elmira College Archives, Gannett-Tripp Library, Elmira, New York.
210. "J. Elizabeth Hotchkiss, Ph.D.," *Elmira Telegram*, July 1, 1894.
211. "The Mayo Wedding," *Elmira Daily Gazette and Free Press*, April 18, 1895, 5.
212. "The Signs of the Times," *Elmira Daily Gazette and Free Press*, 1895 Christmas edition.
213. "Women and Studies," *Elmira Daily Gazette and Free Press*, July 10, 1895.
214. "President, a Woman," *Elmira Daily Gazette and Free Press*, January 4, 1896, 3.
215. "Miss Jeanie Jewell Hotchkiss," *Brooklyn Daily Eagle*, September 7, 1902.

Chapter 15

216. Undated and unattributed article in the "Bob Mack" biography file at the Chemung County Historical Society.
217. For discussions of black minstrel troupes, see: Robert Toll, *Blacking Up: The Minstrel Show in Nineteenth-Century America* (Oxford: Oxford University Press, 1977); Karen Sotiropoulos, *Staging Race: Black Performers in Turn of the Century America* (Cambridge, MA: Harvard University Press, 2008); Mel Watkins, *On the Real Side: A History of African American Comedy from Slavery to Chris Rock* (Chicago: Chicago Review Press, 1999); and Yuval Taylor and Jake Austen, *Darkest America: Black Minstrelsy from Slavery to Hip-Hop* (New York: W.W. Norton & Company, 2012).
218. Brunson III, *Early Image of Black Baseball*, 164.
219. "A Minstrel Gone to Rest," *Owego Evening Blade*, January 22, 1885.
220. "The Original Georgias," *Fort Scott Daily Monitor* (Kansas), November 16, 1877, 4.
221. "The Georgia Minstrels," *Reno Gazette-Journal*, October 1, 1878, 3.
222. "Bob Mack's Rooster," *Brooklyn Union*, May 4, 1883.
223. *Brooklyn Daily Eagle*, December 17, 1882.
224. "Bob Mack's Rooster."
225. "Grand Opera House," *Brooklyn Union-Argus*, December 19, 1882.
226. "A Dying Rooster," *Indianapolis News*, April 19, 1883, 2.
227. *Jamestown Evening Journal*, May 2, 1883.

228. *New York Mirror*, 1883.
229. *Jamestown Evening Journal*, November 17, 1884.
230. "Death of Bob Mack, the Minstrel," *Oswego Times and Express*, January 23, 1885.
231. Errol G. Hill and James V. Hatch, *A History of African American Theatre* (New York: Cambridge University Press, 2003): 124.

Chapter 16

232. *Watkins Democrat*, July 26, 1888.
233. "John Lawes a Famous Fat Man," *Elmira Telegram*, June 14, 1914.
234. "Heaviest Corpse on Earth," *Cherry Creek News*, July 19, 1889, 1.
235. "Death of a Fat Man," *Buffalo Courier*, June 19, 1889.
236. "Heaviest Corpse on Earth."
237. "The Fat Man's Funeral," *Saint Paris News*, July 5, 1889.
238. "Camera Club Is Collecting Old Pictures," *Elmira Star-Gazette*, November 7, 1913, 18.
239. "Tallest Boy in Whole World in the City for Ball Game," *Elmira Star-Gazette*, May 17, 1909, 2.
240. "Seven-Feet Youth Signs with Barnum," *Elmira Star-Gazette*, May 3, 1909, 3.
241. "Tallest Boy in Whole World in the City for Ball Game," 2.
242. *New Ulm Review* (Minnesota), November 15, 1911, 5.
243. "Second Tallest," *Addison Advertiser*, October 28, 1926.
244. "Corning Moose Won 3rd Place," *Corning Evening Leader*, June 12, 1923, 5.

Chapter 17

245. "Professor Smokeball," *Elmira Daily Gazette and Free Press*, February 9, 1904.
246. "Beirweiller Gave Lonesome Lecture," *Elmira Daily Gazette and Free Press*, September 2, 1903.
247. "From Old Growlers," *Saratogian*, April 20, 1945.
248. "Beirweiller Gave Lonesome Lecture."
249. "Pugilist Cardiff Had Case of Cold Feet, *Elmira Telegram*, March 13, 1910.
250. *Elmira Star Gazette*, April 13, 1908, 6.

251. "Hail Smokeball," *Elmira Star Gazette*, March 28, 1909, 8.
252. "Smokeball's Plans Get a Bad Setback," *Elmira Star Gazette*, March 31, 1908, 9.
253. "'Professor Smokeball' Crank Lecturer," *Elmira Telegram*, April 12, 1908.
254. "Smokeballs Wants Good Press Agent," *Elmira Star Gazette*, April, 8, 1908, 2.
255. "Shriner's Banquet Is a Round of Fun," *Elmira Star Gazette*, April 8, 1908, 10.
256. "Mystery Still Unsolved," *Elmira Star Gazette*, May 23, 1908, 7.
257. "Phrenologist in Trouble," *Brooklyn Daily Eagle*, September 30, 1908, 18.
258. "Smokeball Is Back with Many Medals," *Elmira Star Gazette*, June 14, 1909, 7.
259. "Professor Smokeball," *Elmira Telegram*, July 23, 1911.
260. "Smokeballs Off for Lecture Tour," *Elmira Star Gazette*, July 25, 1911, 2.
261. "Smokeball Goes to Big Outing," *Elmira Star Gazette*, October 5, 1911, 2.
262. "Smokeballs Back in Town After Prolonged Absence," *Elmira Star Gazette*, April 5, 1916, 9.

Chapter 18

263. *Elmira Daily Gazette and Free Press*, July 10, 1894, 8.
264. "Champions at the Island Rink," *Wheeling Intelligencer*, March 2, 1885, 1.
265 "Fancy Skating," *Elmira Daily Gazette and Free Press*, November 23, 1905.
266. "Elmiran Attended," *Elmira Daily Gazette and Free Press*, September 12, 1905.
267. "Thomas Grant Welsh," *Elmira Telegram*, September 17, 1905.
268. "Welsh Hears Story of Graft About County Building," *Elmira Daily Gazette and Free Press*, December 5, 1906.
269. "Supervisors Approve Report of the Building Committee," *Elmira Daily Gazette and Free Press*, December 8, 1906.
270. "Scott Welsh, Actor, Singer, Is Dead at 56," *Elmira Star-Gazette*, April 20, 1931, 15.
271. "Displayed Fine Work," *Elmira Telegram*, February 24, 1895.
272. "Scribes See Colleague on the Stage," *Fourth Estate*, November 6, 1920, 19.
273. *Elmira Daily Gazette and Free Press*, August 24, 1901, 8.
274. "Scott Welsh Making Good," *Elmira Star-Gazette*, February 11, 1913, 11.

275. "Gee, It's Great to Be Home," *Elmira Star-Gazette*, June 8, 1916, 7.
276. "Joe Welsh Ends His Engagement," *Elmira Telegram*, July 23, 1916.
277. "Announce Vaudeville Feature for Ambulance Corps Carnival," *Elmira Star-Gazette*, June 11, 1917, 13.
278. "Actor's Wife a Suicide," *New York Times*, July 15, 1921.
279. *New-York Tribune*, July 17, 1921, 14.
280. "Welsh Detective for Third Time in Mystery Film 'Whispering Wires,'" *Cortland Standard*, February 26, 1927, 11.
281. "Scott Welsh, Actor, Singer, Is Dead at 56."
282. "Jansen," *Daily Herald* (Adelaide, Australia), July 15, 1912, 2.
283. *Sunday Times* (Perth, Australia), August 4, 1912, 17.
284. *Alton Evening Telegraph*, December 29, 1905, 1.
285. "About Hunting's Circus," *Elmira Telegram*, September 10, 1893, 7.
286. "Mrs. Welsh to Take Part," *Elmira Daily Gazette and Free Press*, February 8, 1893, 5.
287. "Jansen Show, Touring the World, Prospers Under Good Management," *Player*, February 23, 1912, 22.
288. "Elmiran Has Chance to Wed Genuine Chinese Princess," *Elmira Star Gazette*, December 31, 1912, 4.

BIBLIOGRAPHY

Newspapers and Magazines

Addison Advertiser
Albany Atlas and Argus
Albany Express
Alton Evening Telegraph
American Poultry Journal
Amsterdam Daily Democrat
Auburn Argus
Brooklyn Daily Eagle
Brooklyn Union
Buffalo Courier
Buffalo Express
Cherry Creek News
Corning Journal
Corning Leader
Cortland Standard
Daily Standard (Adelaide, Australia)
Deruyter Gleaner
Detroit Free Press
Elmira Daily Advertiser
Elmira Daily Gazette and Free Press
Elmira Star-Gazette
Elmira Telegram
Fort Scott Daily Monitor
The Fourth Estate
Geneva Courier
Genoa Tribune
The Gentleman's Magazine
Gloversville Daily Leader
Havana Journal
Hornellsville Tribune
Indianapolis News
Jamestown Evening Journal
Medina Tribune
Naples Record
New Ulm Review
New York Mirror
New York Press
New York Sun
New York Times
New-York Tribune
Owego Evening Blade
Owego Record

Oswego Times and Express
Pacific Coast Fancier's Monthly
The Player
Port Jervis Tri-State Union
Reliable Poultry Journal
Reno Gazette-Journal
Rome Daily Sentinel
Saint Paris News
Saratogian
Schuyler County Democrat
Steuben Courier
Sunday Times (Perth, Australia)
Syracuse Daily Courier
Syracuse Journal
Syracuse Post Standard
The Tennessean
Troy Daily Times
Watkins Democrat
Watkins Express
Waverly Free Press
Weekly Standard (Raleigh, NC)
Wheeling Intelligencer
Williamsport Sun-Gazette

Circular of the American Aelloscope Company. Rochester: Wm. S. Falls, 1866.

Dutcher, William. *The Labrador Duck: A Revised List of the Extant Specimens in North America*. N.p., 1891.

Gregg, W.H. *Revised Catalogue of the Birds of Chemung County.* Elmira, NY: G.H. Wheeler, 1880.

Philo, Edgar Woodruffe. *The Philo System of Progressive Poultry Keeping.* N.p., 1910.

Collections at the Chemung County Historical Society's Booth Library and Archive

American LaFrance Collection
Asa LaFrance Biography File
Bob Mack Biography File
Eldridge Park Collections
Henry Clum Biography File
Poultry Review, March, April, June, July, August and September 1908.
Thomas and Jeanie Hotchkiss Papers, MC72 A and MC79 A

Collections at the Elmira College Archives, Gannett-Tripp Library, Elmira, NY

Elizabeth "Bessie" Hotchkiss collection: SL:14:3 and SL:14:4.

Secondary Sources

Beisel, Nicola. *Imperiled Innocents: Anthony Comstock and Family Reproduction in Victorian America*. Princeton, NJ: Princeton University Press, 1997.

A Biographical Record of Chemung County, New York. New York: S.J. Clark Publishing Company, 1902.

Brunson, James E. III. *The Early Image of Black Baseball: Race and Representation in the Popular Press, 1871–1890*. Jefferson, NC: McFarland and Company, 2009.

Chapin, David. *Exploring Other Worlds: Margaret Fox, Elisha Kent Kane, and the Antebellum Culture of Curiosity*. Amherst: University of Massachusetts Press, 2004.

Chilton, Glen. *The Curse of the Labrador Duck: My Obsessive Quest to the Edge of Extinction*. New York: Simon & Schuster, 2009.

Cokinos, Christopher. *Hope Is the Thing with Feathers: A Personal Chronicle of Vanished Birds*. New York: Penguin Group, 2000.

Derry, Margaret E. *Art and Science in Breeding: Creating Better Chickens*. Toronto: University of Toronto Press, 2012.

First Water: A History of American LaFrance. N.p.: American LaFrance, 1982.

Fitzgerald, Deborah Kay. *Every Farm a Factory: The Industrial Ideal in American Agriculture*. New Haven, CT: Yale University Press, 2003.

Gallagher, Peg. "Moonstruck." *New York Alive*, March/April 1986.

Hill, Errol G., and James V. Hatch. *A History of African American Theatre*. New York: Cambridge University Press, 2003.

Hilpert, John M. *American Cyclone: Theodore Roosevelt and His 1900 Whistle-Stop Campaign*. Jackson: University Press of Mississippi, 2015.

Horowitz, Helen Lefkowitz. "Victoria Woodhull, Anthony Comstock, and Conflict over Sex in the United States in the 1870s." *Journal of American History* 87, no. 2 (2000): 403–34.

Huggins, Kelli. "'Learn to Make Poultry Pay': The Philo National Poultry Institute and the Business of Birds." *Chemung Historical Journal* 60, no. 4 (June 2015).

Marvin, Keith. "The Wizards of West Second Street." *Automobile Quarterly* (Fall 1965).

McGrain, Todd. *The Lost Bird Project*. Hanover, NH: University Press of New England, 2014.

Sotiropoulos, Karen. *Staging Race: Black Performers in Turn of the Century America*. Cambridge, MA: Harvard University Press, 2008.

Spajic, Igor. "The Hungerford Rocket Car." *Restored Cars*, nos. 139 and 140 (March/April 2000).

Stein, Geoffrey N. *Daniel and Floyd Hungerford: Rocket Power, Interstellar Travel and Eternal Life.* Albany: New York State Education Department, 2013.

Strasser, Susan. *Waste and Want: A Social History of Trash.* New York: Holt Paperbacks, 1999.

Taylor, Eva C. "Hungerford's Rockets." *Chemung Historical Journal* 20, no. 2 (December 1974).

Taylor, Yuval, and Jake Austen. *Darkest America: Black Minstrelsy from Slavery to Hip-Hop.* New York: W.W. Norton & Company, 2012.

Toll, Robert C. *Blacking Up: The Minstrel Show in Nineteenth-Century America.* Oxford, UK: Oxford University Press, 1977.

Watkins, Mel. *On the Real Side: A History of African American Comedy from Slavery to Chris Rock.* Chicago: Chicago Review Press, 1999.

Weisberg, Barbara. *Talking to the Dead: Kate and Maggie Fox and the Rise of Spiritualism.* New York: Harper San Francisco, 2004.

ABOUT THE AUTHOR

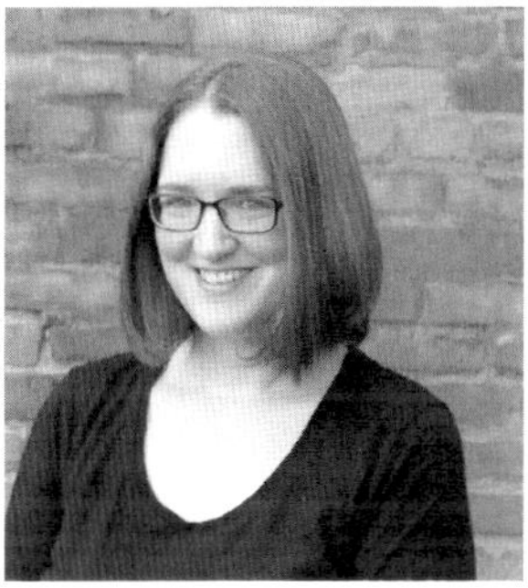

Kelli Huggins is a historian and museum educator with a master's degree in history and a certificate in museum studies. She has written articles for various history publications and has won awards for her research and museum work. Kelli likes her history quirky and frequently works on the history of human-animal interactions. She champions historical oddballs and those forgotten over time.